Old Concord

At Meriam's Corner

Old Concord

By

Allen French

With Drawings by
Lester G. Hornby

WILDSIDE PRESS

Published by
Wildside Press, LLC
P.O. Box 301
Holicong, PA 18928-0301 USA
www.wildsidepress.com

Wildside Press Edition: MMIII

Preface

THIS book, while primarily designed to present the points of chief interest in the historical and literary associations of Old Concord, may also be depended upon for its accuracy. Its historical matter I have drawn from the Concord histories of Lemuel Shattuck (1835) and Charles H. Walcott (1884), from the Concord Social Circle Memoirs, from the writings of Grindall Reynolds, and from the publications of the Concord Antiquarian Society, chiefly those by the late George Tolman. For facts concerning Concord's literary notables I have drawn principally upon their own writings. The

Preface

book also contains material from Concord tradition and family knowledge, not to be found in print. For help in verifying my statements, and for supplying me with much matter previously unknown to me, I am much indebted to my neighbors Dr. Edward Waldo Emerson, Judge Prescott Keyes, and Mr. Adams Tolman. I am also greatly obliged for the courteous help of the librarians of the Concord Free Public Library, and I desire to express my thanks for permission to quote directly from the publications of the Concord Social Circle, Houghton Mifflin Company, and Charles Scribner's Sons.

ALLEN FRENCH.

Concord, Massachusetts.
June, 1915.

Contents

Illustrations

Illustrations

Old Concord

Retrospective

I

THE best point from which to begin to see Old Concord is from the narrow northern end of the Square which lies at the center of the town. Here, from the sidewalk in front of the rambling buildings of the Colonial Inn, one sees stretching away an oblong grass plot of scarcely more than half an acre, with a granite obelisk in its middle. Beyond the oblong, across a strip of roadway, is a grassy oval, from which rises a flagstaff. These open spaces constitute the Square at Concord, Massachusetts, still a center of town life, but more than that, a goal of pilgrimage from everywhere. Here New England farmers and housewives come to attend lectures or town-meeting or church, and to carry on many of the public functions of their lives. But here also come Southerner and Westerner; here come even Englishman and German, Japanese and Hindu, to worship for a day at shrines not yet forgotten.

A road runs round the Square, and at its farther

— the southern — end, its two parts converge into a broad street which seems to narrow as it bends to the left and disappears on its way to Lexington. Its two conspicuous buildings are at its right: first a low, red, hip-roofed structure, the ancient Wright Tavern, where Pitcairn stirred his brandy; then, rising above it, the white Unitarian church, around whose site cluster many memories. As the eye travels from these to the opposite side of the street, and so back along the left of the Square, one sees first a dwelling, then a little burying-ground that climbs a hill, the Catholic church, the opening of Bedford Street, the big red-and-brown Town Hall, and the square, buff Court-house. Or looking from the church and tavern along the right side of the Square, one sees first the beginning of the Milldam (Concord's short business street, closely lined with stores), then the neatly planted open space of the Middlesex Grounds, then the priest's residence, the Catholic parish house, the brick Masonic Lodge, and the new Christian Science church.

Across the Milldam and around the Square move quiet trade, pleasant social life, the town's simple business; and except in winter there ebbs and flows here the tide of tourists in livery carriage or automobile, on bicycle or on foot. But still standing at this northerly end of the Square, one can leave these commonplace modern matters, and can call up visions of many changes.

In 1850, or thereabout, the town was very different. Only a few years before, Bronson Alcott had brought his family to Concord, so he tells us, from up-country on an ox-sled. So much for simple traveling in the middle of the century. But the railroad had just come to Concord too, competing with old Deacon Brown's stage-coach that ran tri-weekly to Boston, and with the stage-lines to the west that, before the railroad, carried to or through Concord as many as four hundred passengers a week. On the Middlesex Grounds stood then the Middlesex Hotel, many-columned, three-storied, spick and span, and overflowing, in its season, into the four other prosperous hostels which the town maintained. For the county court came here twice yearly for long sessions; and the lawyers, their clients, the uniformed court officers, and the various hangers-on, with their inevitable bustle, gave the Square the appearance of holding a fair. Here in the crowd the future Doctor Jarvis, a lank boy with an unforgettable voice, sold the gingerbread of his father the deacon (baked under the building which had been, and would be again, Wright's

Tavern) and received in change the counterfeit quarter-dollar which cut sadly into the day's profits. Years after, in a Boston bookstore, the voice revealed him to his deceiver — not a sharper, but another boy, and very hungry — who abated in trade the twenty-five cents, as conscience money. The Square's only formal planting in those days was an oval grass-patch that broke the line of Bedford Street and the Milldam. No obelisk was as yet to be seen, and wheel tracks crisscrossed the untended space where it was later to stand. The buildings of the Colonial Inn were then three private residences, in the right hand one of which, where the Thoreau family had been brought up, still lived the spinster sisters, aunts of Henry Thoreau. The nucleus of the Christian Science church was then a private house; the Masonic lodge building had but lately been the school where the young Thoreau tried his famous experiment in flogging. There was then no Catholic parish in Concord, and the priest's residence was the "county house," the dwelling of the keeper of the jail that stood behind — of which also Thoreau had his taste. On the site of the Catholic church stood the "green store" which supplied ropes and disguises to the young men of the town, when they marched down Lexington

The Unitarian Church

Retrospective

Road one dark night, intending to do a service to Ralph Waldo Emerson. The Court-house was just building in 1850; the Town Hall was not erected till five years later. The Universalist church, which since has vanished, then stood hard by in Bedford Street; it took its origin at the meeting called by posted notice, summoning all persons in favor of the universal salvation of all mankind to meet at Bigelow's Tavern and choose officers. The Unitarian church was in the early glory of its new belfry, for it was but a few years since the building was turned to face Lexington Road, the Grecian portico added, and the slender spire removed. And Concord, not then a suburb but a self-sufficing community, was a fine example of a thriving shire town.

As for tourists in the fifties, there were none. To be sure, strangers came, but they were mostly visitors of certain residents who all belonged to the peculiar class of writers. The usefulness of some of these inhabitants the town took the liberty of doubting. The names of the freeholders among them were marked on the town map of 1852. "R. W. Emerson," whose house was at the junction of Lexington Road and the Cambridge Turnpike, the town indeed knew well. Was not his grandfather here at the time of the Fight, he who urged the militia to take their stand in the town itself ? This William Emerson built the Manse a few years before he went away to die in the Revolutionary War; and periodically young Ralph and his brothers had visited here in the old house, under the kindly eye of old Doctor Ripley, who married their grandfather's widow. And since 1832, when he came here to live, the philosopher had brought credit to the town by his writings — except for his antislavery notions. Yes, Emerson the town knew well, and on the whole was proud of him.

"J. Thoreau's" name was marked, on the map, against a house on Main Street. He too was a dependable person, and had brought up his family as a respectable man should. But his son Henry turned out odd enough, even if his name were known as far as New York, or even England. He had never made his way in the world; he would earn only enough to keep him, though he was smart enough when he improved his father's pencil-making machinery. But having done that, he went out to Walden Pond and spent two years alone in a shanty. What could be done with such a man ?

Thus it was plain to the town that some of the Concord folk whom strangers came to see were rather queer. There was, for example, this "Nathl.

Retrospective

Hawthorne," whose name stood on the map against the Lexington Road house which Mr. Alcott sold when, following another of his strange ideas, he went to Boston. Mr. Hawthorne was becoming celebrated, so people heard, from his book about a scarlet letter; but he was so unsocial that he took to the woods when people came to visit him. Didn't he use to stand in his garden at the Manse and dream, in full sight of the road, instead of working? The man lived in a dream! When Emerson's little son showed Mr. Hawthorne some pictures of this very Square, he asked what place it was! And he had passed through it hundreds of times.

Also this "W. E. Channing," who owned a house on Main Street opposite Thoreau's: he might be a poet, but he was as unsociable as Mr. Hawthorne, and he walked more miles in the fields and woods than any other man besides Henry Thoreau.

Naturally the town looked askance at the strangers who came to visit these men. Some of the visitors were certainly famous, and were inoffensive enough. But others were mighty queer. Those men with long hair, and women with short, and cranks with schemes to make the world over, or with diets, or methods of dress — Why, they swarmed like bees around Mr. Emerson's door, and the poor man could hardly get rid of them. Transcendentalists they called themselves — and no one could give a satisfactory meaning to the word!

And there was surely smuggling of slaves through Concord by. means of the Underground Railroad. Of course the men who took the risk were so cautious that it would be hard to prove anything against them; but still, the town had its opinions. The Thoreaus were abolitionists, parents and children; it was said that Henry hid slaves in his hut at Walden. It was curious that when strange negroes took the west-bound train, Henry Thoreau was very likely to board it with them, buying tickets to Canada but returning too soon to have used them himself. Miss Mary Rice, the odd little spinster who planted the lilies on John Jack's grave, was said to have had a cubby-hole built in her house for the special purpose of hiding runaways. And Edwin Bigelow the blacksmith, who was on the jury for trying those who took the slave Shadrach away from his jailers in Boston — *Edwin Bigelow was the very man who harbored Shadrach in Concord and drove him to Leominster on his way to freedom!*

It was all a very dubious business and clearly against the law. It was even a very ticklish matter

Retrospective

for young Mr. Frank B. Sanborn to have John Brown, the Kansas abolitionist, here in Concord to give an address. The frontiersman slept with a big knife at his side and a brass-bound pistol under his pillow. Next would come United States marshals with warrants to arrest Concord citizens.

But though the grumblers did not so recognize it, the mid-century period was a great one in Concord's development. Great thoughts were being conceived, great books being written, by her citizens. And even those who took the conservative stand, shaking doubtful heads at antislavery and the Underground Railroad, were slowly being trained to meet the day when, not far ahead, the call should come for Concord's soldiers. The only thing to depress them then was the rumor that the company was not to be allowed to go. To be sure, old David Buttrick had wise advice for his sons: "Don't go now. This ain't to be a short war, and the time will come when *they'll pay a bonus.*" And Humphrey Buttrick seemed to have taken the advice. He had a family to maintain, and withdrew from the company, to the noisy scorn of a neighbor. But when the time came to march, Humphrey presented himself, and the scorner was not there; so his uniform was sent for, and Humphrey marched away in it. And David, standing by his ox-team, waved good-by to all his sons.

In the fifties, Concord seemed one large family, intimately acquainted with each other's affairs. There may have been family quarrels over politics, over town offices, but they left no bad blood. Even the question of temperance, which came nearer home than slavery, made no feuds. The nearest to a show of ill-feeling was roused by Doctor Bartlett, who through his practice knew most of the evils of drink, and who attacked the rumsellers unsparingly. Once his opponents took the nut from his wheel, causing him a fall; and once they cut off the tail of his horse and slit his chaise curtains to ribbons; but horse and chaise the doctor continued to drive as they were, to the shame of his persecutors. A "character" the old doctor may have been throughout the fifty-seven years of his Concord practice; but he left an enviable record of public and private service. And it needed character to rise to note in that place and time of strong personalities, bred on New England soil, and with all the Yankee characteristics not yet smoothed out by prosperity and outside intercourse. The lives of these men, written in Concord's Dictionary of Biography, the Social Circle Memoirs, permit an intimate view of a community kindly and helpful, yet also shrewd, witty, penetrating in criticism, and unsparing in attack.

Yet on the whole those were easy-going times. Because Puritanism had gone by, and the stern call of war had not yet come, there was still tolerance for the two great inherited social evils, slavery and intemperance. Ways of living were very simple, in spite of new improvements in stoves, and lamps, and imported luxuries. Easy-going days those were, when the temperance lecturer was invited by the committee to the hotel, and flip was passed around. Easy-going when the judge, finding that the jailer had taken his prisoners out haying, adjourned court till the work should be done. Especially easy-going when the bank cashier left the safe open when he locked the front door, and so during his lunch-hour, one fine day, lost the little sum of three hundred thousand dollars.

But let us go back another fifty years. In 1800 there was no railway; over the wretched roads (for turnpikes were not yet general) struggled but a single coach; and the one daily mail and the weekly newspaper were uncertain in their arrival. Concord lived very much by itself. Though the county courts sat here, in a smaller and quainter building, the volume of business was slight. There was no level space for the Town Hall and Bedford Street; but the flagpole on the ridge was already in danger from the cutting in the gravel pit which would finally grow big enough to make room for them. The Meeting-house then faced the Square; over its portico was a graceful spire whose removal the older inhabitants were later so much to regret, offering in vain to replace it. By the tavern stood the single little fire-engine house that served the whole town. The Milldam was really a milldam, and though the stores that lined it cut off the view of the pond which business was soon to abolish, the old mill was still in active use. The Middlesex Hotel site held the Jail Tavern, hiding the old stone jail. Beyond the County House was the wooden schoolhouse where the brick one was later to stand. The dwellings at the end of the Square were used for trade, having little shops either in their fronts or in sheds close by. The Square was unplanted; it was the Common then, and the only visible object that broke its surface, except for the elm on its eastern side — in those days used as a whipping-post and even to-day holding somewhere within its bark the staple to which offenders were tied for punishment — was the town pump.

The Old Tree at the Town Hall

Retrospective

Other differences could be seen in the town. There was much more woodland, and the oaks on top of Lee's Hill, until recently owned by the traitor himself, had just been cut for the frigate which they were building in Boston, to be named the *Constitution.* And the life in Concord was very simple. There was but one church, at which all religious people assembled twice on Sunday for three-hour services, "the old, cold, unpainted, uncarpeted, square-pewed meeting-house," which Emerson remembered so well, "with its four iron-gray deacons in the little box under the pulpit, with Watts' hymns, with long prayers rich with the diction of ages, and not less with the report like musketry from the movable seats." There were no lectures, and the new library society must wait another thirty-five years before it accumulated nine hundred volumes. There were almost no amusements, scarcely even the pleasure of shopping, for Concord stores were very few. But to make up for this, Concord people were very busy with the work of procuring their necessaries.

To begin with, a century ago, almost every one in Concord, even the mechanics, the one doctor, the one lawyer, and the minister himself, made much if not all of his living by farming. This meant hard and continuous labor, extending even to the women. To preserve from spoiling, all beef and pork that was not immediately eaten must be salted or cured, for there was no ice. So every dwelling had its brine barrel, and its smoke-house for the curing of hams. There were candle-molds hanging in each kitchen, in which the housewife could make four, six, or a dozen candles at a time. There were other implements also: the hackle, the flax-comb, the wool-cards, the dye-pot, the wool-wheel, and the spinning-wheel; and in most houses there was still the loom. And these, which were used for making the clothes for the family, meant work for every one. The flax was grown on the farm, the wool was raised there, and the men (a hard-working, hard-drinking race) cut the crop and sheared the sheep, in the proper season. A little cotton was bought or bartered. The women did the rest. The rotted flax was hackled and combed, the cleaned wool was carded into its little white rolls, the women walked miles at the wool-wheel, or sat uncounted evenings at the flax-wheel; they dyed the skeins, set up the loom, wove the woolen cloth, the linsey-woolsey, the linen sheets and spreads and curtains. Fine work they did, these ancestresses of ours, with patterns handed down from their grandmothers, or combined from ancient designs, expressing here, and here only, their sense of the beautiful.

And for the children, the life was not easy. Early and late they had to help their elders. At astonishingly early ages the little girls were set to making the samplers which nowadays we collect but cannot imitate. School perambulated like the cobbler, from district to district; and the teachings were only of the rudiments. The pleasure of reading was lacking, for there were no magazines or story-books, and even for the grown-ups there were no novels. Tired little folk nodded by the fireside while the parents gossiped or discussed theology, for the Unitarian controversy was upon the land. Or the children crept up-stairs to their chilly rooms, begged for the warming-pan between the cold sheets, and drew the bed-curtains close about. Romantic it may be, seen through rose-colored spectacles a hundred years later; but at the time, the life was sad and drab.

One feature of the period was the prohibition of Sunday traveling. Deacons and other such severe persons took it upon themselves to watch the roads and to halt all travelers between Saturday and Sunday sunset. Of Deacon White, who lived at the corner of the Square and guarded Lowell Road, they tell that on a Sunday morning he stopped a teamster on his way home and forbade further progress. The teamster tied his horses at the deacon's gate, sat (smock frock beside broadcloth) at church in the deacon's pew, ate of the deacon's dinner, sat again through the afternoon service, partook of the deacon's supper, until at last the good man saw with relief that the sun was down and bade his guest proceed. Years later Samuel Hoar also was diligent in stopping travelers. One farmer, ruefully studying the destruction caused in his crops by a tornado, found his only relief in the ejaculation: "I wish this tornado had come last Sunday. I should have liked to see whether Sam Hoar would have tried to stop it!"

Another fifty years back, to 1750, reveals less change. Yet there were two notable differences, for folk talked of their king and looked with friendly interest upon traveling redcoats, asking them of the war with France. People spoke of England as "home." George the Third was not to come to the throne for ten years; and the days of Whig and Tory, and of the fight for independence, were a generation in the future. Concord was smaller, even more isolated and provincial, with the houses clustered in little villages. The Square was shape-

The Old Colonial Inn — Deacon White's Corner

Retrospective

less and neglected; the Town House, the meeting-house (barn-like, yet destined to harbor Harvard College), the new little tavern, and the jail, were the chief public buildings. There was the yearly excitement of "seating the meeting-house," when the parish committee was driven to its wits' end, and the town stirred to its depths, by hurt and angry feelings. But the home drudgery, the lack of amusements, the sadness and drabness, were more marked than later.

When we get to the year 1700, we find one other factor in life: the unforgettable dread that the Indians may swoop down, as was done to Concord's neighbor in Philip's War, scarcely fourteen years before, and as would be done to Deerfield yet. The daily life was very laborious. And Concord was very primitive, since the little meeting-house was used for church, for town-meeting, and for a court when necessary. As for hotels or taverns, there were none, nor stores, nor much more than bridle-paths for the pedlars who alone brought finery to town.

Sixty-five years farther back, and there was — wilderness.

But the place was not all forest. The three hills were wooded, also the ridges that ran here and there, and much of the land that lay fifteen feet or more above the river level. Yet Concord's Great Meadows were large, open spaces, almost free from floods and fairly well drained, where (among the sweet fern and straggly brush) stood each year patches of maize. These were fertilized — five herring to a hill — with the fish that came up the Musketaquid River each year in spawning time. The corn was planted and tended and reaped by the squaws that came from the encampment under the hill called Nashawtuc. And the fields had once been seen by a white man who came with Indian guides, and made marks in a book, and disappeared in the direction of the settlements on the coast.

And then, late in the fall of this year that the white men called sixteen hundred and thirty-five, out from the fringe of woods came more white men on to the great meadows. They had no guides, which accounted for the hardships of their journey hither, for their torn clothes, scratched legs, and boots marked with the slime of the swamps; but they walked all over the meadows with Tahatta-wan the Musketaquid chieftain, shook hands with him on some bargain, and seemed pleased. And not far from the little brook which the Indians dammed with a fish weir, and which perhaps the beavers first dammed centuries before, where was a mill site, and a sunny hillside close by, these white men marked out plots of ground, and promising to come again, plunged into the forest, this time with a guide to show the shortest way to the settlements.

In the spring they came again, and more men with them, and their wives and children and goods, over the rough road that had been opened from Watertown. This was a notable venture — that men from civilized England should settle here, twenty miles from the coast, twelve from navigable water, surrounded by savages. But the need of the day was for farming land, and all else was forest; so here came these adventurers, led by two ministers and by a soldier turned trader, to bargain with the Indians under the great tree on what was some day to be Concord Square. The white women huddled together at one side, their children beside them. The squaws stood silent at another. And beneath the tree sat the chiefs and the Squaw Sachem and the medicine man, opposite the white men who were no whit less grave; and they smoked the peace-pipe and discussed terms, until at last Master Simon Willard, rising in his place, and "poynting to the four quarters of the world," declared that the white men had bought three miles from that place, east and west and south and north. The red men agreed, and wampum and hoes and hatchets were given; and every Indian there stared with admiration at the medicine man, who stalked about in a suit of clothes, a hat with a white band, shoes, stockings, and a great coat. But the white men noted that this bargain had been made with the best of good feeling, and that among their own company there was very close fellowship; so for these two good reasons they changed the name of the place from Musketaquid to Concord. There was no thought that a war would some day begin there; only the hope that the peace of God would dwell in that place.

The first year for the white men was a hard one. In the side of the sunny hill they made dugouts to last them until harvest, while they wrestled with the root-encumbered soil, got out their timbers from the woods, and built, first of all, the meeting-house. The frail roofs leaked, fare was scanty, the summer heat was new to them, the wolves got all the swine, and the only meat they had was bought from the Indians — venison and "rockoons." But by winter their houses were framed and boarded in, and a little crop was harvested. Concord had indeed to cut its bread very thin for a long season, but the beginning had been made.

Of all the little company, our sympathy must go out strongest to Peter Bulkeley, the leading minister. Willard, his right-hand man, was a soldier and used to hardship. John Jones, his colleague, lost heart and went away. But Bulkeley, gently nurtured, fought the fight through. He was a man of education; he had stood well in Puritan circles, until forced by Charles I to leave his pulpit, a martyr to his opinions. Moreover, being a man of property and therefore taxable, he was forbidden to emigrate. But he took the risk and slipped away. If here in Concord meadows he saw a likeness to his fertile Bedfordshire and its winding streams, the resemblance was but slight. Here he dwelt by the Square in a log house; his land was stubborn and unfruitful at first; his money brought him no income. Nay, he spent freely more than four of the six thousand pounds which he brought to the colonies, in the necessary outlay for those who came with him to Concord. Friends he had in Boston and Cambridge, but he might have been leagues from them as well as miles, for all he saw of them. He wrote: "I am here shut up, and do neither see nor hear." His wife frightened him by a sickness, and anxiously he watched over her in the uncomfortable attic, until at last he could report that again she "began to come down into the house." Besides all this, he bore his people's burdens. The first of Concord's many books contains his own published sermons, in which he exhorts his people to holiness, evidently seeing nothing else to stay them in their troubles.

Those troubles were not slight. Sheep could not live unless cattle had first been pastured on the land, and the cattle did very poorly on the meadow grass. Apparently there were wet seasons when the land was flooded and the crops suffered. The people could not maintain their two ministers (for Bulkeley, no longer rich, needed a salary); there was even talk of abandoning the enterprise, and the elders from Boston were called in conference on the matter. Finally there came "a discord in the church of Concord," caused apparently by Bulkeley's "pressing a piece of charity" against the stiff conscience of his colleague. So Jones led away "the faint-hearted souldiers among them," and all we can guess of the ins and outs of the matter is from Bulkeley's statement that by it he came: "1. To know more of God. 2. To know more of himself. 3. To know more of men."

Relieved of its excess of ballast, the enterprise

now showed promise of success. Minor troubles
were easily managed, sometimes by the peremptory
measures of those days. Poor Mr. Ambrose Martin
called the church covenant "a human invention,"
and was fined ten pounds. To secure the fine, the
officials took property which sold for twenty pounds;
but the offender could not be persuaded to accept
the remainder, even though he came to want. The
tender conscience of Bulkeley led him to urge on
the governor a remission of the original fine; but
stern Endicott refused, and "our poore brother"
went destitute to his grave.

The Indians never threatened Concord; they
were, at least in early times, rather to be considered
as childlike dependents. As they failed to understand that they had sold their fish-weir with the
land, a second bargaining seems to have been necessary, in order that the white men might be free to
build their mill upon the brook. And so the beginning of our Milldam was made. The personal
habits of the Indians grieved and sometimes vexed
their white brothers, until a sort of treaty was
drawn up, by which the Indians agreed to submit
themselves to fines and other simple punishments
for ordinary misdemeanors. But since the occasion
was too good not to improve for both religion and

morality, the Indians were induced to promise to "improve their time," to labor after "humilitye," to wear their hair "comely like the English," to give up greasing themselves, not to howl and paint themselves when mourning, and to knock before entering an Englishman's house.

Nevertheless, smile as we may at these simple matters, there was a pathetic note in the Indians' request that they be not forced to remove far from their friends at Concord, but that they be allowed to remain near by, in order to hear the word of God, and not to forget to pray. So a settlement was granted them in Nashoba, now Acton, but a few miles away.

There was in early days a beginning of our Square. Soon after Bulkeley's time, it became common land. And we may be sure, as we look at it, that Bulkeley trod it, and John Eliot, the apostle to the Indians, through whose aid, doubtless, the Concord Indians were so tamed. And Winthrop and Dudley, brothers-in-law, must have come here, for they owned land just outside the town and gave their name to the boundary stone in the brook in the east quarter,— the Two Brothers.

And hard times passed. The shapeless common, the dam at the mill, saw the empty houses filled, more people at meeting, prosperity. Bulkeley could at last know that his great venture had succeeded. His neighbors could look forward to a secure future. Emerson mirrored their minds when he wrote:

"Bulkeley, Hunt, Willard, Hosmer, Meriam, Flint,
   Possessed the land which rendered to their toil
   Hay, corn, roots, flax, hemp, apples, wool, and wood.
   Each of these landlords walked amidst his farm,
   Saying, ''Tis mine, my children's and my name's.
   How sweet the west wind sounds in my own trees!
   How graceful climb those shadows on my hill!
   I fancy those pure waters and the flags
   Know me, as does my dog: we sympathize.'"

Military Affairs

II

AS geography is the handmaid of strategy as well as of trade, let us, before we leave this post at the north end of the Square, master so much of the plan of Concord as is necessary for a clear understanding of its famous Fight. Coming from Boston by way of Lexington, Lexington Road (closely bordered for a mile on the right by a steep ridge) leads into the Square at its farther end. From the near left-hand corner, Monument Street leads out again to the North Bridge, less than a mile away. These two streets mark the essential route of the British; the ridge, which less steeply borders Monument Street also, was a factor in the doings of the day. Out of the Square, again, the Milldam leads to the right, and by way of Main Street takes travelers to the South Bridge. In early times, there were no other bridges in the town, and no other streets led from the Square. The Town House (its site marked by the present memorial stone at the west of the Square) Wright's

Old Concord

Tavern, the Meeting-house, and the brick mill at the end of the Milldam, were the chief buildings.

For some years previous to 1775, trouble had been brewing in Massachusetts. Boston had experienced its Massacre and its Tea-party, and was filled with the king's soldiers. Against them the spirit of resistance was growing in the colony. The line of cleavage in the people, dividing Whig from Tory, showed itself very plainly in Concord. It even cut into families. Daniel Bliss, the former pastor of the town, had been a stout old loyalist; but his children took different sides. Phebe, a woman of strong character, married her father's successor, young William Emerson, first of the name in Concord, but of Bulkeley blood, and a defender of the rights of the colonies. Phebe's brother Daniel took the other side. A lawyer, he upheld the law; the son-in-law of a prominent Tory, he was strengthened by family influence. His house stood on Walden Street; the dwelling must have been nearly opposite the present post-office, though then there were no buildings between it and the mill-pond. Bliss was one of the justices of the Court of Common Pleas, with the rest of whom he was forced to promise to discontinue its sittings. He had even to submit to being deprived

[38]

of his tea, and had to be careful where he bought any of his supplies; for Concord, like other towns, not only refused to buy goods imported from England, but even threatened a boycott against all who did buy any.

Bliss is well remembered for his share in a striking scene that took place in the old meeting-house. Conventions were frequent in those days; they were held in the big church, and at one of them Bliss seized his chance to express his opinion, and to utter his warning, on the course which the Whigs were pursuing. His address was a good one, driven home with forensic skill, wit, and biting sarcasm. The wealth and power of Britain made her invincible; the fringe of colonists along the coast could do nothing against her might; they were treading a dangerous way, and should turn back before they were crushed. At the end of the speech, there was such a silence that Bliss must have believed himself successful. Then, since the older men did not speak, slowly there rose from his seat a young man in homespun, at the sight of whom the eyes of all the Whigs brightened. He began slowly, but as he gained confidence, his halting words began to come as freely as those of Bliss. His ideals were higher, his appeal more thrilling.

A Worcester delegate, watching the frowning and fretting Bliss, asked, "Who is that man?"

"Hosmer, a mechanic."

"A mechanic? Then how comes he to speak such good English?"

"Because he has an old mother who sits in the chimney corner and reads English poetry all the day long; and I suppose it is 'like mother like son.' His influence over the young men is wonderful, and where he leads they will be sure to follow."

And follow they did. The response to Hosmer's speech showed Bliss that the struggle must come. There was left for him only to show that he believed in his own words.

This final test came to another Tory earlier than to Bliss. On the farm where once dwelt "Simon Willard, one of the founders of Concord," lived Joseph Lee, the town's physician. Everything is now changed about his place, even to the very name; for Lee's Hill is now Nashawtuc, two bridges make useless the doctor's ford, and many modern residences dot his acres. Lee was a man born for opposition and hot water; he had seceded from the parish, forming with others what was derisively called the Black Horse Church, because it met in the tavern of that name; and when the original cause of quarrel had been removed, he made as much uproar in trying to return as ever he had done in seceding. Such a man was likely to take an original path in revolutionary troubles; and he did so.

There came to town the news that Gage, the governor in Boston, had seized the provincial powder and cannon, and might shortly do — nobody knew what. The occasion of reproving him, and at the same time of removing some of the new unpopular officers, was too good to be lost. From all towns the militia companies, some actually under the belief that Boston had suffered a second Massacre, hurried toward Cambridge. Planning a night march, Ephraim Wood, one of Concord's most important men, invited the doctor to go, — perhaps as a test.

"My heart is with you," quoth the doctor, "but I cannot go."

Yet at early darkness the doctor crossed the ford; and when the company returned from its successful journey, it was discovered that he had been to Cambridge in advance of them. Summoned and questioned — was it before one of those impromptu meetings in the Square, to which the town was then much given? — he admitted that he had given warning of the coming of the militia.

The sequel was the humiliating declaration which Lee publicly signed. "When I coolly reflect on my own imprudence, it fills my mind with the deepest anxiety. I deprecate the resentment of my injured country, humbly confess my errors, and implore the forgiveness of a generous and free people, solemnly declaring that for the future I will never convey any intelligence to any of the court party, neither directly nor indirectly, by which the designs of the people may be frustrated, in opposing the barbarous policy of an arbitrary, wicked, and corrupt administration."

Concord meeting-house became for a while the center of interest for the whole of Massachusetts. Let us remember that in those days the old church stood lengthwise to the road, without bell or cupola or external ornament; but that it was roomier even than at present, having two galleries that accommodated all members of the Provincial Congress which, late in 1774 and again early in 1775, met here to plan the rebellion. Here the Congress passed its resolve to stop the payment of taxes to the king; here it began the treasonable action of raising and equipping an army. And in Concord began to accumulate those military stores which the royal governor would have to seize if he wished to cripple his disloyal subjects. It was at Concord, therefore, that his first blow must be struck.

Foreseeing the great emergency, the province increased its military strength. Its ancient militia comprised every able-bodied man; but now from these were drawn new companies to make a mobile force of young men, ready to spring to arms, and to march as far and as swiftly as might be needed. It was Concord which first created their form of oath, "to hold ourselves in readiness at a minute's warning with arms and ammunition." So the Minutemen first came into being. At worship or at work, their arms were always at hand.

The comic now intruded. Wearing disguises which no Yankee could fail to penetrate, trudging on foot, two British officers came to spy out the land. They sketched a map of the roads, saw what they could of the preparations for defence, and asked their way to the house of Daniel Bliss. A woman pointed across the Milldam to the house that looked on the pond. A very comfortable dinner they must have had with Bliss, glad as they were to get out of the public gaze.

But Bliss can scarcely have been easy in his

mind, knowing that his guests had been marked to his door. First the woman who had guided them came, weeping because of her townsmen's threats against her; then came a message for Bliss himself: he should not leave the town alive!

"What," asked his guests, "are the Yankees ugly? Will they fight?"

Bliss pointed out the window. "There goes my own brother. He will fight you in blood up to the knees."

"Come away with us, then," urged the officers. "We are armed and can protect you."

So by Lexington Road the three stole out of town in the dusk, and Bliss never saw Concord again. For him, comedy had become tragedy; and for the country, the whole great drama at last was turning grimly earnest. Lexington Road, the Square, and the Milldam, were to witness more than this pathetic exit.

Paul Revere came frequently from Boston, bearing messages from Joseph Warren to Hancock and Samuel Adams and the other provincial leaders in the Congress. On the fifteenth of April Revere brought word that the British would move soon. Much too slowly it was borne in upon the guardians of the stores that it was foolhardy to wait longer.

Military Affairs

But when the word was given, Concord sprang to tasks which had been designated at least a month beforehand. Horses were hitched, carts trundled on the highway, and at noon on the eighteenth of April, powder and ball were loaded up for their journey to places of greater safety. The "alarm company," true to their oath, must remain on the spot; but the other men were busily driving the carts away.

The work was too great to be done quickly, but it was eagerly pushed. The powder must first have been saved, for none whatever was captured. But it must have been plain that the rest of the stores — cannon, shot, bullets, and food — were in danger. Over the roads, never too good, and always soft in spring, the heavy carts labored. The Square must have been a busy place till late at night, and peace came slowly to the town.

Then the call of war came early. Young Doctor Prescott, who had been visiting his sweetheart in Lexington, and who was returning in company with Paul Revere, bearing the fateful news of the coming of the British, barely escaped when Revere was captured by a patrol of English officers. By a roundabout route he came to Concord with the alarm, roused the guard at the Court-house, and told his news. Alarm guns were fired, and the bell was tolled. It is said that the first man to appear in response was the minister, William Emerson, his gun on his shoulder. And in a little while the whole of the alarm company was there, parading on the Square.

Wright's Tavern was the focus of excitement for many hours, the small, square, hip-roofed building, in those days without its present ell. Such organization as could be maintained was centered there, where the officers and selectmen were accustomed to meet, and where now it was natural to go for consultation. The work of saving the stores was continued as best it could be, but the absence of most of the teams made it impossible to cart away all of the remaining deposits. Some of them were concealed near by, under hay or brush, or in the woods; but at the mill and the malt-house the barrels remained unhidden. One careful soul saved the church silver by throwing it into the soap-barrel at the tavern, whence it emerged so black that no one but a silversmith could polish it.

The men who had yesterday gone away with the teams at last began to come back with their muskets; the Minutemen from Lincoln arrived; some few came, as individuals, from other towns. The

The Wright Tavern

commanders of this little body marched them to the liberty pole on the hill, to wait there while a detachment was sent to reconnoiter. Down Lexington Road this company marched, past the spot where Hoar had housed his Indians, past the place where, in imagination, Hawthorne put the house of Septimius Felton on that day, past the end of the winding ridge that flanked the highway, and out upon the Great Meadows toward Lexington. And then, says private Amos Barret, who was of the company, "we saw them coming." He leaves us to imagine the scene as viewed from Meriam's Corner: the Minutemen in homespun halting, the British in their scarlet, gold, and flashing steel advancing upon them across the level, sunlit meadow.

The Minutemen marched back, their drums and fifes playing defiantly — "and also the British. We had grand musick," writes the simple private. But the matter was more seriously viewed by the leaders under the liberty pole, to whom flying messengers bore word of the overwhelming strength of the regulars. One fiery soul spoke out.

"Let us stand our ground!" cried the minister. How they must have loved him for it!

But there were strategists at the council, cunctators, delayers. Time would conquer these invaders before night. The regulars came in sight, the grenadiers on the road below, the light infantry advancing as flankers along the ridge, fiery eager at the sight of the liberty pole and its defenders. But the best possible disposition had been made of the stores, the town was practically empty of its inhabitants, and there was nothing to fight for. And so the militia withdrew across the North Bridge, to wait reinforcements on the slope of Punkatasset Hill. As they passed the Manse, the minister dropped out of the ranks, staying to defend his little family.

It was the British who now occupied the Square. Their commander, Smith, sent guards to the two bridges, and a detachment across the North Bridge. In the village, the remaining troops were busy, ransacking all possible hiding-places and destroying what they could. They found two cannon and knocked off the trunnions; they rummaged out a quantity of wooden spoons and intrenching tools and burnt them on the green; at the malt-house, they found the barrels of flour, broke some of them open, and rolled the rest into the mill-pond.

But the barrels thus submerged were found, when drawn out, to have protected their contents very well. Bullets flung into the pond were, when salvaged, quite as good as ever. The quantity of flour stored near the mill was saved by a trick. Among them were some bags and barrels of the miller's own, and when questioned by an officer, he put his hand on these. "This is my flour," he said. "I am a miller, sir. Yonder stands my mill. I get my living by it. In the winter I grind a great deal of grain, and get it ready for market in spring. This is the flour of wheat, this is the flour of corn, this is the flour of rye; this," and again he touched his own property, "is my flour; this is my wheat; this is my rye; this is mine." The officer studied his countenance, and then, remarking that the miller seemed too simple to play a trick, left the barrels untouched.

Beyond the mill, and beyond the burying-ground on Main Street, stood Bigelow's Tavern, where was stored a chest of papers and money belonging to the treasurer of the province. As the soldiers were about to search the chamber in which it lay, a maid remonstrated, declaring that the room was hers and contained her property. Again the partial truth concealed a fact, and the chest was left untouched.

On the Square, beside the Town House whose

site is marked by a tablet, lived Martha Moulton, "widow woman," seventy-one years old, whom the general flight of neighbors had left alone with an old man of more than eighty. A politic soul she proved herself, submissive to the soldiers who demanded water, and to Major Pitcairn and the other officers who sat on her chairs on the grass, directing their men. She had even scraped a little favor with them, so as to chat, "when all on a sudden they had set fire to the great gun carriages close by the house," and she saw smoke rising from the Town House, "higher than the ridge." Bravely she expostulated with them, would not be rebuffed by sneers, pointed out the sure damage to the row of buildings, and standing with a pail of water in her hand, "put as much strength to her arguments as an unfortunate widow could think of," and so touched Pitcairn's heart. The fire was extinguished by the soldiers who set it, and for her services Martha Moulton was later awarded the sum of three pounds by a grateful province.

So far as is known, Amos Wright stayed by the tavern to which, though his occupancy was the shortest in its history, he gave his name. He had been a schoolmaster; later he was called captain:

but on this day his business was to protect his property by ready and obliging service to its temporary possessors. For Smith made it his headquarters, and from it issued his orders. And when from the North Bridge came the report that the militia were gathering on the hill beyond in threatening numbers, Smith may be pictured as leaving the tavern to march on foot, "very fat, heavy man" as he was, at the head of the reinforcing detachment. Perhaps he wanted the relief of walking, after twenty miles of unaccustomed riding; but at any rate, so a grumbler among his subordinates recorded in his diary, "he stopt 'em from being time enough."

Pitcairn was left in command at the tavern. His fortune connected him closely with American history at this period, for he fell bravely at Bunker Hill. "Amiable and gallant," an opponent wrote of him; he was beloved by his men and respected by his adversaries. But he is best known by a remark which he made as he stood, it is interesting to think, in front of the tavern, with his critical eye upon the men who were still at their work of burning the American supplies. Who reported the remark? No one so likely as the tavern keeper, who brought him the glass of brandy and water —

and sugar — which the major jovially stirred with his finger.

"I hope so to stir the Yankee blood this day."

Was it then that he heard, from the direction in which Smith had disappeared, the distant crash of musketry?

Satisfaction first, at the short sullen roll of the regular volley. These homespuns were again, as at Lexington, as at Boston five years before, being taught their lesson. But next came, for the first time, startling as the noise of a gigantic watchman's rattle shaken by a warning hand, the sharp reverberation of the scattering reply.

What hasty orders shouted and reëchoed, what snatching up of weapons, what hurried forming of ranks in the Square!

Meanwhile, the detachment sent to the North Bridge had taken up its several duties. Three companies pressed on beyond the bridge, and under the guidance of one of those officers who had come to visit Daniel Bliss, sought the house of Colonel James Barrett, still standing on Barrett's Mill Road. Barrett was the commander of the militia, a man of sixty-four, disabled from much marching, but active on horseback. The stores were largely in his charge, and he had been very busy in re-

moving them. On the retirement of the militia
from the town, he had hastily ridden home, given
directions concerning stores to be hidden on his
place, and had once more departed to join his men.
Those at the farm had been working hard. The
bed of sage was lifted, cannon wheels were planted
underneath, and the herbs replaced. Other material was hidden under hay and manure. In the
garret were flints, balls, and cartridges, stored in
open barrels, in the tops of which, having no time
for removal, the womenfolk put a few inches of
feathers. Most valuable, however, were certain
cannon. These were hastily taken to the field, a
furrow plowed, and the guns laid in it; then they
were concealed by turning another furrow over
them. This work was finished while the regulars
were in sight, advancing on the farm.

Mrs. Barrett was equal to the emergency. Com-
posedly she gave leave to search the buildings, gave
food and water to the men, refused to provide
spirits to a sergeant. Thereupon Captain Parsons,
the commander of the party, forbade the man to
drink: he needed to be fit for duty, for there was
bloody work ahead, on account of the men killed
at Lexington. Mrs. Barrett refused pay for her
provisions, saying: "We are commanded to feed

our enemies." When they threw the money in her lap, she remarked: "This is the price of blood." The men found some gun carriages and piled them for burning, near the barn. At this Mrs. Barrett expostulated, and the material was removed to a safer place. Of her son the captain demanded his name and ordered him seized, to be sent to England for trial. "He is my son," said Mrs. Barrett, "and not the master of the house," and so he was released. As the gun carriages were for the second time about to be lighted, the noise of firing was heard from the bridge, and Captain Parsons called his men together for the retreat.

In order to understand what happened at the bridge, we need to remember that in those days the present highway bridge did not exist, and that the old bridge, now in its *cul-de-sac*, carried the main road. Though now the approach is more closely shaded by trees, the place is otherwise the same. From its bend the sluggish stream flows under the simple structure; the meadows lie open to the sun; seldom are signs of industry in view. There is not even the plash or murmur of quick water.

To this abode of peace, then, came the soldiers. Captain Laurie, holding the bridge, disposed his men according to his best skill. One company he

The Old Elisha Jones House — The House with the Bullet Hole

posted, mistakenly, across the river, where the statue of the Minuteman now stands. Another company he sent to the top of the ridge past which he had come. Everything goes to show that the country was then not so wooded as to-day, and that men thus posted could see much. His third company was, for a time at least, at the Elisha Jones house, which stands opposite the Manse, one of the very oldest houses in the town. In outline it was much the same as to-day, with its two stories and hip roof, and its shed connected with the house. The soldiers swarmed in its dooryard and drank at its well; they did not search the building, nor did they suspect that its owner was in its cellar with a loaded musket, ready to protect not only his family, but also tons of the fish and beef which the soldiers had come from Boston to destroy.

The soldiers appear also not to have molested the Manse. There the minister remained with his family, one of whom (that Mary Moody Emerson to whom the philosopher was later to owe so much) used to boast that she was "in arms at the Fight." But there was no joking at the time; the minister could have seen very little good cheer in his view of the redcoats on two sides of his house.

The militia, on leaving the town, had crossed the

bridge and waited on Punkatasset Hill for the reinforcements which speedily came. More Concord
men returned from their journeys with the stores;
and singly or in companies, men came in from
Bedford, Acton, Westford, Chelmsford, and Carlisle.
Joseph Hosmer, whom we have seen defeating
Daniel Bliss in debate, was made adjutant of the
muster. Growing more confident as his strength
increased, Colonel Barrett ordered the provincials
down to the neighborhood of the house of his major,
Buttrick. The militia and Minutemen formed at a
spot marked to-day by a tablet in the wall of Liberty
Street, whence the riflemen among them might have
dropped their bullets among the guard at the bridge.

At this movement of the provincials, the regulars
were alarmed. Captain Laurie called in his two
outposts, and the three companies formed at the
head of the bridge, still mistakenly on the same
side as the militia, without protection of any sort.
The captain sent to Smith his summons for reinforcements, while the Americans still lingered behind the breastwork of a wall, not ready to take
the responsibility of an attack. A great responsibility! For they were still subjects of the king,
bred in the Englishman's dislike of change, and
open to the vengeance of the strongest power on

earth. The news from Lexington had not yet certainly reached them. And so they hesitated, the higher officers consulting with some of the civilians as to what should next be done.

It was now, not long after nine o'clock of that fine morning — the sun still as bright as when prophetic Samuel Adams, at dawn in Lexington, had called it glorious; the grass, in that early spring, mid-leg deep in the field below — it was now that Hosmer, the adjutant, saw large clouds of smoke rolling up above the town. His soul took fire; he went to the council of his superiors and demanded, pointing to the smoke: "Will you let them burn the town down?"

The captains immediately begged to be sent against the bridge. Smith, of Lincoln, offered to dislodge the British. Davis, of Acton, said, "I haven't a man that's afraid to go." The responsibility of the order rested with Barrett, the colonel, and manfully he took it. He ordered Buttrick to lead his men at the bridge, with the caution not to fire unless fired upon. For every provincial in Massachusetts was drilled in the precept that the king's troops must shed the first blood. The Acton company took the lead in columns of twos; presently Captain Brown's Concord company pressed up abreast of it; behind was the second Concord company, and then the remaining troops, their order directed by the mounted colonel. In front marched Buttrick, and with him Lieutenant-colonel Robinson of Westford, to whom Buttrick had offered the command, but who preferred to march as volunteer. Thus they bore down upon the bridge.

At the first movement of the Americans, Captain Laurie, perceiving the weakness of his position, hastily withdrew his men across the bridge, and formed them clumsily once more, the companies one behind the other, "so that only the front one could fire." At the captain's order, some of the men began to take up the planks of the bridge, an act quite of a piece with all that he had done, since he thus would endanger the retreat of the detachment at Colonel Barrett's. Buttrick, raising his voice, shouted to the British to desist.

At this, two or three shots were fired by the British into the river, signal or alarm guns, to which the Americans paid no attention. A shot was fired at Buttrick himself; it passed between him and Robinson, and wounded two men behind. Davis, the Acton captain, stepped to one side to be clear of his men, and prepared to fire, when immediately the British volley rang out. Davis fell, and with him one of his men. Some few were wounded, the rest untouched by the bullets that went overhead. Said Amos Barrett: "The balls whistled well."

Over in the Manse the minister, his soul on fire, had but one dread: that the volley would not be returned.

He need not have doubted. Buttrick sprang from the ground as he turned to the ranks. "Fire, fellow-soldiers, for God's sake, fire!" The order was doubtless modified by the company commanders. Says Barrett: "We were then all ordered to fire that could fire and not kill our own men." The minister heard the response and saw the result. Leaving two of their privates dying on the ground, with half their officers wounded, and many of their men, the regulars retreated in haste, around the bend in the road and past the Elisha Jones house.

Here Jones, roused from his concealment in the cellar, threw up an upstairs window to fire on the retreating redcoats. But his wife clung to him, showed him the danger to the family, and took away his gun. Then Jones, in scornful triumph, showed himself at the door of his shed, to sneer at the beaten troops as they crowded by, some binding up their wounds, some aiding their limping comrades. One of the British, observing him, fired hastily as he passed. The bullet passed through the wall 'at his right and glanced out through the rear into the hillside. The front wall shows its hole to this day.

The Americans, coming in pursuit, saw the fugitives join Smith's party. After some hesitation, the regulars retreated. Smith thus left Captain Parsons and his detachment to their fate. The provincials could have intercepted them. But not yet had the rebels realized that, as has been said, while the men to whom Buttrick gave his order were subjects of King George, the men who fired and who pursued were citizens of another country. Not yet did they feel that this was war. The three companies were allowed to pass on their hasty retreat, the guard from the South Bridge came in, and the whole force of regulars was gathered in the village.

Here they were too strong for the Americans; and besides, they could burn the town. But time was still working for the militia. Therefore nothing was done by them while Smith, by futile marchings and countermarchings, displayed, as the minister wrote in his diary, "great fickleness and inconstancy of mind." The British commander was perhaps waiting for the reinforcements for which he had sent; but at last, being but too well aware that the country was aroused against him, and that he must start soon if he wished to reach Boston at all, about noon he began his retreat.

The troops marched out of the town as they had entered, by Lexington Road. For a mile this is bordered by the ridge which we have repeatedly noticed; and to prevent attack from this vantage point, Smith sent his flankers along it. It was on this ridge, where Hawthorne later wore his path, that he set the scene of Septimius Felton's duel with the British officer.

"While the young man stood watching the marching of the troops, he heard the noise of rustling boughs, and the voices of men, and soon understood that the party, which he had seen separate itself from the main body and ascend the hill, was now marching along on the hill-top, the long ridge which, with a gap or two, extended as much as a mile from the village. One of these gaps occurred a little way from where Septimius stood. . . . He looked and saw that the detachment of British was plunging down one side of this gap, with intent to ascend the other, so that they would pass directly over the spot where he stood; a slight removal to one side, among the small bushes, would conceal him. He stepped aside accordingly, and from his concealment, not without drawing quicker breaths, beheld the party draw near. They were more intent upon the space between them and the main body than upon the dense thicket of birch-trees, pitch-pines, sumach, and dwarf oaks, which, scarcely yet beginning to bud into leaf, lay on the other side, and in which Septimius lurked.

"[*Describe* (says Hawthorne's memorandum) *how their faces affected him, passing so near; how strange they seemed.*]

"They had all passed, except an officer who brought up the rear, and who had perhaps been attracted by some slight motion that Septimius made, — some rustle in the thicket; for he stopped, fixed his eyes piercingly towards the spot where he stood, and levelled a light fusil which he carried. 'Stand out, or I shoot,' said he.

"Not to avoid the shot, but because his manhood felt a call upon it not to skulk in obscurity from an open enemy, Septimius at once stood forth, and confronted the same handsome young officer with whom those fierce words had passed on account of his rudeness to Rose Garfield. Septimius's fierce Indian blood stirred in him, and gave a murderous excitement.

"'Ah, it is you!' said the young officer, with a haughty smile. 'You meant, then, to take up with my hint of shooting at me from behind a hedge. This is better. Come, we have in the first place the great quarrel between me, a king's soldier, and you a rebel; next our private affair, on account of yonder pretty girl. Come, let us take a shot on either score!'

"The young officer was so handsome, so beautiful, in budding youth; there was such a free, gay

[66]

petulance in his manner; there seemed so little of real evil in him; he put himself on equal ground with the rustic Septimius so generously, that the latter, often so morbid and sullen, never felt a greater kindness for fellow-man than at this moment for this youth.

"'I have no enmity towards you,' said he; 'go in peace.'

"'No enmity!' replied the officer. 'Then why were you here with your gun amongst the shrubbery? But I have a mind to do my first deed of arms on you; so give up your weapon, and come with me as prisoner.'

"'A prisoner!' cried Septimius, that Indian fierceness that was in him arousing itself, and thrusting up its malign head like a snake. 'Never! If you would have me, you must take my dead body.'

"'Ah, well, you have pluck in you, I see, only it needs a considerable stirring. Come, this is a good quarrel of ours. Let us fight it out. Stand where you are, and I will give the word of command. Now; ready, aim, fire!'

"As the young officer spoke these three last words, in rapid succession, he and his antagonist brought their firelocks to the shoulder, aimed and fired. Septimius felt, as it were, the sting of a gadfly passing across his temple as the Englishman's bullet grazed it; but, to his surprise and horror (for the whole thing scarcely seemed real to him), he saw the officer give a great start, drop his fusil, and stagger against a tree, with his hand to his breast."

Past the scene of this imaginary duel, past the ridge itself and out into the open, the regulars marched. At Meriam's Corner the meadow begins, and there comes in the old road from Bedford. As the British left the corner, down from the ridge came marching the front rank of the pursuing Americans, while the Bedford road was filled with the alarm companies from Reading and Billerica. The British rear-guard halted, turned, and fired on their pursuers. The Americans responded so accurately that the regulars fled again. "When I got there," says Barrett, "a great many lay dead, and the road was bloody."

Another mile, and the British were out of Concord territory; but in that mile they got their taste of that which was to come. From wall and thicket, from hill-top and wood, bullets came from unseen marksmen. Here and there were flitting figures; but no regiment stopped the road, nor did any visible body of troops present such a challenge as the honor of the regulars would allow them to accept. Men dropped in the ranks, Pitcairn was wounded and lost his horse, the officers had to turn their swords upon their own weary and demoralized men to keep them from headlong flight, and it is said that Smith would have surrendered before reaching Lexington could he have seen any one of sufficient rank to whom to offer his sword. And

The Monument of 1836, and across the Bridge the "Minute Man"

when at last in Lexington the fleeing redcoats met the relieving column under Lord Percy, they flung themselves for rest on the ground, their tongues (in the words of their own historian) hanging out of their mouths like those of dogs after a chase. A little rest under the protection of Percy's cannon, fifteen miles more of flight and chase, and the troops reached their own lines, not again to leave them until they were driven from Boston, eleven months later.

Such was, for Concord, the day of the Concord Fight. The numbers engaged were small, the losses on either side were comparatively unimportant, but the act was immensely significant. The history of a continent had changed.

But as we look at French's noble statue of the fine young Minuteman leaving the plow in the furrow to start with his rifle for the beginning of a great war, we must not allow ourselves to suppose that individual impulse guided or decided the events of the day. True, the citizen soldiery was from its youth accustomed to the rifle, and the harrying tactics of the pursuit necessarily depended on the skill of the separate men. But even this was guided by method, and the action of the day had been foreseen and planned long in advance. The organiza-

tion of the Minutemen was months old; throughout the province the regimental rosters were
complete; each company knew its meeting-place and
the shortest route to the line of the British march.
And at Concord the wise strategy of the day was
decided by the elder officers; there was nothing
haphazard in either the delay or the attack. The
courage and initiative of the Minuteman are indeed
worthy to be commemorated in bronze; but we
must remember that his less striking qualities, his
cool foresight, and his wise and thorough prepara-
tion, in reality decided the day.

In the fight and pursuit, no Concord man was
killed. Of the town's four wounded, three were its
captains. Immediately began the long experience
of divided families, the sending of supplies, the care
of the wounded. Of those who went away to death,
the finest was William Emerson, who as chaplain
went to Ticonderoga, sickened, and died on his way
home. At home the two prominent men were
Ephraim Wood and Joseph Hosmer, whose work in
regulating the community and in gathering stores
for the army was many times worth their possible
services at the front. During the year of Boston's
siege, Harvard College was located in Concord, the
recitations being held in the Court-house and the

church. Concord stories of that dreary war period
are few. Said one wary individual after the Fight,
"For myself I think I will be neutral these times."
His indignant neighbors took his name from the
jury box and denied him his rights as a citizen.
The estate of Daniel Bliss was confiscated. And
Joseph Lee came a second time under the unfavor-
able notice of his townsmen. He was ordered to
keep the bounds of his own farm, being warned that
"if he should presume to go beyond the bounds and
should be killed, his blood be upon his own head."

The canny doctor stayed carefully at home and
managed to survive the war, in spite of the habit of
his neighbors to discharge their guns in the direction
of his house whenever the spirit moved them.

The rest of Concord's military history is the same
as that of all the New England towns which sent
their men to later wars. Her glory must always
center at the North Bridge. Yet, curiously enough,
for a long time the place was neglected. The highway was changed, the bridge removed, interest in
the spot was suffered to lapse, and not until 1836
was a memorial set on the spot where the British
had stood : the weathered granite monument which,
impressive in its plainness, bears its proud inscrip-
tion commemorating the first forcible resistance to

British aggression. By the wall lie buried the two British privates killed in the Fight, over whom for more than a century and a quarter there was no other memorial than the words "Grave of British Soldiers" carved on an unfinished slab. The present slate tablet, with the verses from James Russell Lowell's fine poem, was placed in position only recently. In 1875, the centennial of the Fight, the bridge was rebuilt, and on the farther bank, where the militia had stood, was erected Daniel Chester French's noble Minuteman. But the monuments subdue themselves to the landscape. The rustic surroundings of the bridge shade and soften bronze figure and granite shaft; only in the spring floods does the river change its placid mood; and the visitor to the scene of Concord Fight, the spot where America altered her destiny, is tempted to muse upon a scene of peace rather than to kindle his spirit in memory of war.

Graves of British Soldiers

Chiefly Literary

III

TO fit Concord's history with her geography, let us trace once more the lines of her streets, in order to point out the buildings of chief interest. Radiating, as the streets do, irregularly from the Square, they make it difficult for the visitor to reduce them to a system, or even for Concord residents to tell, offhand, the points of the compass. It is therefore better, at the opening of our chapter, to explain at once the general plan of the town, more carefully than was needed for the story of the Fight, yet simplified from the intricacies of modern Concord. With this in mind, Concord's literary history can be more clearly followed. So again let us begin at our north end of the Square.

At the left hand, by the Court-house, we have already noted the beginning of Monument Street, which for long was the only road to towns lying to the north. (Lowell Road, starting at our right, is a short cut, generations younger.) Monument Street curves away over a gentle rise; it borders fertile meadows, so here lay some of the earliest farms. And here, where the old road took a sharp turn to the right, to meet the river, two of the ancient houses face each other, — the Manse among its fields, and the Elisha Jones house at the foot of the ridge. Between them the modern highway runs directly onward to the later bridge.

Again from the left hand of the Square, between the Town Hall and the Catholic church, starts Bedford Street, not old, but much traveled by the tourist on his way to Sleepy Hollow Cemetery. Immediately behind the Town Hall is the yellow house in which Elizabeth Alcott died. A short stretch of Bedford Street, up a gentle rise, leads to the gate of the oldest portion of the cemetery. Or following the curve of Bedford Street a couple of hundred yards farther, one comes to the gate that leads to Sleepy Hollow itself.

At the end of the Square, we have seen the beginning of Lexington Road, with Wright's Tavern and the Meeting-house at its right. These two buildings are of Revolutionary rather than of modern interest; unfortunately the handsome church is only a reproduction of the old building burned in 1900. Opposite them stands the picturesque old stucco dwelling now appropriately fitted up as the

The Old Chapter House of the D. A. R.

chapter house of the Daughters of the American Revolution. The wide street stretches on, past the plain old house that now contains the collection of the Antiquarian Society, to the turn where still stands the Heywood house. Round this turn and past this house swept, so many years ago, the flashing battalions of King George, coming on their fruitless errand. As we go past this Heywood corner there opens up, across a gently sloping field to the right, the view of a white house behind a line of lofty pines and chestnuts. It stands near the road behind another screen of trees; its plain dignity and refinement seize the attention and stir imagination. This is the Emerson house, sheltered yet approachable, pleasing with its fine background of fertile meadow fringed with distant trees.

Lexington Road winds gently on, over a little rise where another fine old house stands below the ridge which, — higher or lower, but always close at hand, — borders the highway at the left. Beyond this Moore house, the road dips and sweeps a little to the left; and here in a bay, as it were, of the highway, and in a hollow made by a little recession of the hill, stands a brown house behind two great elms, a large house, homelike although old-fashioned, hospitable even if unoccupied. This is the

"Orchard House" of the Alcotts, now a museum to their memory. The ridge rises, the trees descend and gather thickly, some even stand close to the road as if to hide a house that stands crowded between it and the hill. It is Hawthorne's "Wayside," which the wood seems almost to draw into its dark depths. The effect is carefully preserved by "Margaret Sidney" (Mrs. Daniel Lothrop), the present owner of the property. But the little cottage close beyond rejects the spell, its white cosiness defying gloom. The tablet in front of the enclosed trellis tells that here was bred the Concord grape. On winds the road below the ridge, until, a mile and a half from the village, the hill abruptly stops. Here the Great Meadows stretch into the distance, the road strikes out across their sunny width, and a tablet in the wall reminds us that here, at Meriam's Corner, was the field of a bloody encounter.

Returning to the Square, we take the fourth street, the Milldam. At the end of its short length, Walden Street branches abruptly to the left. Speedily quitting the clustered buildings of the town, this street leads across a mile of Concord's level meadows until it begins to climb a wooded slope. The ascent is Brister's Hill, named for the bygone freedman whose cabin and spring near the foot of the hill Thoreau described. In the woods to the left lies "Fairyland" with its pond, beloved in Concord for its natural beauty and its earliest skating. Members of the "Walden Pond Association" (those members of the literary circle of fifty years ago whose Sunday walks took them to nature rather than to church) knew "Fairyland" well. To the right of the road lie Walden woods, and a quarter of a mile farther along the road, after reaching the top of the rise, the view of the pond itself opens through the trees. Walden lies in a deep basin, wooded, irregular, very pleasing. It has no inlet and no outlet; it is often (a natural curiosity) higher in summer than in spring. Except for the ancient settlement whose decay Thoreau chronicles, and a deserted picnic ground, only the naturalist himself has built on Walden's shores, and even his cabin has gone. Bathers come sometimes to Walden, or solitary fishermen; but mostly its expanse is silent and deserted. To reach the cairn that shows the site of Thoreau's cabin, the visitor, after climbing Brister's Hill, should take the first road to the left, and turn first to the left and then to the right. He will find himself by the shore of Thoreau's cove, with the cairn above him in its little hollow.

Old Concord

From the point where Walden Street began, Main Street continues the line of the Milldam. The house beyond the bank building, setting back from the street, tradition claims to have been a blockhouse; certainly the thick walls of the original structure were once suitable for defence. Next lies an old burying-ground, perhaps as ancient as the one upon the hill. At the fork where Sudbury Road branches to the left, stands the Public Library, a brick building of the Gothic type, soon to be remodeled. Opposite, on Main Street, begins the series of buildings connected with the Hoar family, so important in Concord. And on the left of the street, the third house beyond Belknap, stands the yellow house which Thoreau rebuilt with his father, where he spent his last years, and where the two famous Alcotts, father and daughter, lived in the period of their own decline. Following Main Street farther, Thoreau Street and Nashawtuc Road meet at the next corner; then Elm Street branches off, and leading to the river nearly a mile from the Square, leads also to the house inhabited by Frank B. Sanborn, standing on the right bank. Main Street itself crosses the river by the South Bridge, passes under the railroad track, and shows beyond (the second house on the right) the Alcott "Cot-

The Thoreau-Alcott House

tage." In *Little Women*, this is described as Meg's "Dovecote"; but in fact none of the Alcotts lived in it except at their earliest visit to Concord.

Such, following each road to its farthest important landmark, is the plan of literary Concord. If the visitor mentally will reduce the map of the town to these few elements, he will be able to follow easily the remainder of our story.

The Old Manse comes nearest to connecting Concord's military and literary annals. For while it was built by the martial minister, and while from its windows was seen the flash of the guns at the bridge, it is also closely linked with the names of Concord writers. Its aspect would not prepare one for its distinction. Well withdrawn from the road, with its modest gambrel roof, its weather-beaten clapboards, its partial screen of trees and shrubs, the gray house, as if in melancholy brooding over its past, seems to retire from the wayfarer's gaze. It sets low; there are no wide lawns or ornamental planting to challenge attention: the surroundings of the venerable building still recall the time when its fields maintained its owners. And that is right, for here, if anywhere, have been plain living and high thinking.

Built in 1765, the Manse after eleven years passed

to the ownership of William Emerson's widow, who after two more years married his successor. For sixty-three years Ezra Ripley ruled, as still in his days a minister could do, over a respectful parish. Simple, downright, a believer in his calling and himself, even in his oddities he typified the ancient school of which he was almost the last example. Openly from the pulpit, or privately to the ear of his parishioners, he spoke with the authority of his office, guided by a knowledge that did not come of books, and a kindness of heart that always distinguished him. Not experienced in the ways of the outer world, he could be deceived by any traveling swindler; but in the difficulties and even the etiquette of parochial life, no one had a clearer eye or surer speech. When after a return from a prison term a Concord man made a social call, Doctor Ripley received him kindly; but when a fellow minister appeared Doctor Ripley said to the first comer: "Mr. M., my brother and colleague has come to take tea with me. I regret very much the causes (which you know very well) which make it impossible for me to ask you to stay and break bread with us."

When the highway was changed, and the old North Bridge removed, the abandoned road became a field belonging to the Manse. With this field we may associate two stories of the good old doctor. He took an innocent pride in his possession of the famous ground, and it was his pleasure to have his hired man ask in the presence of guests into what field he would have the cow turned. "Into the battle-field," would be the reply, always effective in bringing conversation to the favorite subject. And it was perhaps in this very field that Emerson, haying with the old gentleman, saw his pleading, almost reproachful glances at the approaching thunderstorm.

"He raked very fast, then looked at the cloud, and said, 'We are in the Lord's hand; mind your rake, George! We are in the Lord's hand'; and seemed to say, 'You know me, this field is mine — Dr. Ripley's, thine own servant!'"

The old clergyman gave back the ancient roadway to the town for the dedication of the monument of 1836, the occasion for which Emerson wrote his beautiful hymn, one verse of which stands engraved on the base of the Minuteman statue of 1875.

Plain speech accompanied Doctor Ripley's tales of the parish, which no man knew better than he. "I remember, when a boy," says Emerson, "driving about Concord with him, and in passing each house he told the story of the family that lived in it; and especially he gave me anecdotes about the nine church members who had made a division in the church in the time of his predecessor, and showed me how every one of the nine had come to a bad fortune or a bad end." At a certain funeral he spoke fearlessly to the inheritor of the family responsibilities, a man whose temptations sometimes overcame him. "There is no man of this large family left but you; and it rests with you to bear up the good name and usefulness of your ancestors. If you fail — Ichabod, the glory is departed! Let us pray." Of sot or spendthrift, of any one in whose conduct there was a flaw, the doctor never hesitated to demand an explanation in order to cure the fault.

In his little study, square, wainscoted, with the beams showing, he must have written thousands of sermons — "it is awful," says Hawthorne, "to reflect how many." The Manse ghost is a fiction of Hawthorne's, who pretended that he heard it sighing, or turning over sermons. "Once, while Hilliard and other friends sat talking with us in the twilight, there came a rustling noise as of a minister's silk gown, sweeping through the very midst of the company so closely as almost to brush against the chairs."

Chiefly Literary

To the Manse came the young Emersons to visit
with their step-grandfather. And it may have
been at the door of the house that the old minister
said to the young Ralph Waldo, on parting after a
bereavement which had severed the last blood-
relationship between them: "I wish you and your
brothers to come to this house as you always have
done. You will not like to be excluded; I shall not
like to be neglected."

Consequently it was to the Manse that Emerson
turned his steps after he had himself withdrawn
from the ministry and was following his new fortunes. "Hail," he wrote here, "to the quiet fields
of my fathers." Here he lived; and here he wrote
the first of his great books, *Nature*. Even after
he had left the Manse for a dwelling of his own,
and after Doctor Ripley's death, he was still a visitor
at the old house, where he was drawn by the enigma
of Hawthorne's personality.

For Hawthorne, not yet famous, had rented the
Manse not many months after the decease of the
old clergyman. Apparently it attracted him from
the first, by its individuality and seclusion. He
describes with gusto the antique character of its
interior and furnishings, and feels secure, in its
privacy, against the passing stranger who from the

road could thrust his head into other domestic circles. Doubtless Hawthorne was attracted by the "most delightful little nook of a study" in the rear of the house, facing west and north on the orchard and the river, its window-panes cracked (tradition said by the volleys at the Fight), and its walls blackened by the smoke of generations. Yet the transformation from smoke and old woodwork to fresh paint and wall-paper delighted him. In July, 1842, he married, and almost immediately brought his bride to the Manse.

The seclusion which he valued at first sight, he enjoyed through three years at the old house. Yet it was a seclusion into which the modern may pry. In the preface to the *Mosses,* and in the published Hawthorne letters and journals, we get a closer glimpse of his household than we can elsewhere get of most others. The character of both the house and the occupants are revealed in this intimate writing. The cold of the winters (when the steam from the wash-tub froze on the servant's hair), the beauty of the summers, the joy in nature, and the more than joy in each other — these are shown in diary and letter. Morbid, we may think, was Hawthorne's shrinking from meeting with visitors. But this seems almost an essential part of his nature.

The Old Manse

Chiefly Literary

Hawthorne was his own workman, split the wood and shoveled the snow, and even, in emergencies, boiled the potatoes "with the air and port of a monarch." Whatever he did, his wife admired him for it, held him in reverence, would not trespass on his time. She had a pretty sense of guilt when the beauty of the sun after a shower made her call him to the window. Idealist as she was (indignant, for example, with the doctor for calling her child "red-headed"), with her many minute touches she draws a very fine picture of her manly husband, not afraid of servile duties, struggling with his art, waiting the slow payment for stories already sold and printed, fretting at debt, and yet jesting, as he watched her mending his old dressing-gown, that he was the man with the largest rents in the country.

But even though Hawthorne loved solitude, the Manse was no hermitage. By persistent kindness new neighbors of the occupants made themselves welcome there. Emerson came often. So many around him were mere echoes of himself, that it refreshed and delighted him to find a man of such individuality as Hawthorne. First of all he noted Hawthorne's striking dignity: his aspect was regal, even when he handed the bread at table. And then

his reticence charmed the philosopher, long accustomed to men of ready speech, so that we see
Emerson changed from his own oracular attitude.

"Mr. Emerson delights in him; he talks to him
all the time, and Mr. Hawthorne looks answers.
He seems to fascinate Mr. Emerson. Whenever he
comes to see him, he takes him away, so that no
one may interrupt him in his close and dead-set
attack upon his ear." So different were the natures
of the two men that neither truly appreciated the
achievements of the other; yet there was between
them from the first a strong bond of mutual interest
and respect.

"It was good," wrote Hawthorne, "to meet him
in the woodpaths, or sometimes in our avenue, with
that pure intellectual gleam diffused about his
presence like the garment of a shining one; and
he so quiet, so simple, so without pretension, en-
countering each man alive as if he expected to re-
ceive more than he could impart." The picture is
unforgettable.

Another visitor to the Manse at this time was
Thoreau. Here were still stronger differences than
before, for the contemplativeness of Thoreau, as
real as that of either of his townsmen, was, as it
were, active, busy, and inquiring. His robustness

kept him moving, and he came to the Manse not so much to visit Hawthorne as to tempt him out upon the river, where according to season they paddled or skated, or rode the great ice-cakes in their sluggish way down-stream. Hawthorne found in him an honest and agreeable ugliness of countenance, and a wild, original nature. Mrs. Hawthorne pictures the contrast between her husband and his two friends when skating on the river below the Manse, Emerson unskilled, Thoreau "figuring dithyrambic dances and Bacchic leaps", and Hawthorne "like a self-impelled Greek statue, stately and grave." The Hawthorne music-box lured Thoreau; he delighted in it. The romancer purchased Thoreau's boat, and as if in mockery of the stream by which (he says) he lived for weeks before discovering which way it flowed, re-christened the boat the *Pond-Lily*. And yet one cannot find that the bond between the two men grew very close, in spite of their journeyings. Thoreau was too strenuous and abrupt for Hawthorne's more leisurely nature.

It was with Ellery Channing, — poet and nature-lover, more of a hermit than any of these friends, because both less able and less willing to express himself, — it was with Channing that Hawthorne took his greatest pleasure out of doors. And if Thoreau has revealed to us the spirit of Walden, Hawthorne more than any one else has written most intimately of the river, in his account of these excursions with Channing.

"Strange and happy days were those when we cast aside all irksome forms and straight-laced habitudes, and delivered ourselves up to the free air, to live like Indians or any less conventional race during the bright semi-circle of the sun. Rowing our boat against the current, between wide meadows, we turned aside into the Assabeth. A more lovely stream than this, for a mile above its junction with the Concord, has never flowed on earth, — nowhere, indeed, except to lave the interior of a poet's imagination. It is sheltered from the breeze by woods and a hillside; so that elsewhere there might be a hurricane, and here scarcely a ripple across the shaded water. The current lingers along so gently that the mere force of the boatman's will seems sufficient to propel his craft against it. . . . At one point there is a lofty bank, on the slope of which grow some hemlocks, declining across the stream with arms outstretched, as if resolute to take the plunge. In other places the banks are almost level with the water; so that the quiet congregation of trees set their feet in the flood, and are fringed with foliage down to the surface. . . .

"So amid sunshine and shadow, rustling leaves and sighing waters, up gushed our talk like the babble of a fountain. The evanescent spray was Ellery's; and his, too, the lumps of golden thought

that lay glimmering in the fountain's bed. . . .
But the chief profit of those wild days to him and
me lay, not in any angular or rounded truth, which
we dug out of the shapeless mass of problematical
stuff, but in the freedom which we thereby won
from all custom and conventionalism and fettering
influences of man on man. We were so free to-day
that it was impossible to be slaves again to-morrow.
When we crossed the threshold of the house or trod
the thronged pavements of a city, still the leaves of
the trees that overhung the Assabeth were whisper-
ing to us, 'Be free! Be free!' Therefore along
that shady river bank there are spots, marked with
a heap of ashes and half consumed brands, only
less sacred in my memory than the hearth of a
household fire."

The hemlocks which Hawthorne here describes
are still a feature of the river. They lie on the
Assabet, only a little way above Egg Rock, the jut-
ting ledge which marks the meeting of this stream
with the Sudbury to make the Concord River.
Near here the ancient Indian encampment stood.
The waters of these rivers are now discolored by
the waste from mills nearer to their sources; but
the banks are just as lovely, and it requires but
little imagination to picture the old "owners of
Musketaquid" lolling under the hoary hemlocks,
or fishing in their shade. Under their many bridges
the rivers glide as sleepily as when Hawthorne en-

joyed their peace; and the wide meadows give vistas, the overhanging trees offer shady retreats, which still tempt nature lovers out upon the waters.

To Concord came occasionally Hawthorne's more distant friends to search him out. Franklin Pierce, Hawthorne's college classmate, was the most notable of these.

Except for the editing of the naval journal of his friend Bridge, Hawthorne's literary work while at the Manse was comprised in the *Mosses*. For a long time he must have been too happy to write: his description of his domestic contentment shows his marriage to have been ideal. But money matters began to press on him, he was much troubled by the slightest burden of debt, and decided to accept a position in the customs service. His years at the Manse, as he glanced back at them, seemed to him very brief. "In fairyland there is no measurement of time; and in a spot so sheltered from the tumult of life's ocean, three years hastened away with noiseless flight, as the breezy sunshine chases the cloud shadows across the depths of a still valley. . . . We gathered up our household goods, drank a farewell cup of tea in our pleasant little breakfast room, and passed forth between the

The Hemlocks

tall stone gateposts as uncertain as the wandering Arabs where our tent might next be pitched."

At the time when Hawthorne first came to Concord, Emerson was already widely known. *Nature*, written at the Manse, had been followed by the Phi Beta Kappa oration and the divinity school address, two public utterances which brought upon him the clamor of shocked conservatives, but also the eager and unquestioning applause of the seekers after new light. These last soon began to flock around him in his new home on Lexington Road.

This dwelling is on the corner of the Cambridge Turnpike. The Emerson acres stretch for a little distance along this road; one field lies across the brook. The house was built in the twenties by a well-to-do Bostonian; it long had the distinction of having the only dry cellar in Concord. When in 1835 Emerson married for the second time, he purchased the vacant house; and bringing his bride to it immediately after his marriage, he lived there until his death in 1882. The building has the simplicity of the best New England architecture, and its dignity also; for the square white house, lacking ornament, its Doric porch-columns and its few moldings almost severe, stands without concealment or pretence. A group of noble pines and chestnuts, with a few younger evergreens, shades it from the sun; there is no other shelter. If the retirement and mystery of the Manse echoes the character of him who made it most famous, the frankness of this other house, tempered always by the restraint of a fine self-respect, equally personifies its even greater occupant. Hawthorne seemed always to withdraw; Emerson came forward with a kindly welcome.

Of all who came to that door, none has left a more vivid picture of the master than Howells, who as a young man sought his acquaintance. He describes the fine old man at his threshold, looking down at his visitor with a vague serenity. Emerson was then about sixty, yet scarcely showed his age in his face of marble youthfulness, refined to delicacy by his high and noble thinking. Howells felt the charm of Emerson's eyes, shyer, sweeter, and less sad than the similarly charming glance of Lincoln. The smile was indeed incomparably sweet, with a quaintness, gravity, and archness which Howells was baffled to describe.

This inscrutableness of Emerson's was a quality inseparable from his insight; but as Howells well understood, it was inseparable also from his kindliness. These qualities showed visibly in his gentle smile, which endeared him to the young people of the village. Says Hawthorne's daughter, speaking of her childhood :

"My earliest remembered glimpse of him was when he appeared — tall, side-slanting, peering with almost undue questioning into my face, but with a smile so constant as to seem almost an added feature, dressed in a solemn, slender, dark overcoat — upon the Concord high-road. . . . It then became one of my happiest experiences to pass Emerson upon the street. A distinct exaltation followed my glance into his splendid face."

And Louisa Alcott has told of her enthusiasm for Emerson, how she brought him offerings of flowers, and sang to him ("*à la Bettina*", but modestly unheard) outside his window.

The interior of the house has often been described. Its famous study, to the right of the front door, contains neither desk nor desk chair; it has the appearance of an ordinary sitting-room, except that one side is lined to the ceiling with books on simple shelves. Yet it is here that Emerson wrote all the books which he published after the year 1835. Sitting in his simple rocker, his writing-pad on his knee, he culled from his many journals, or from his own retentive memory, the golden sentences which go to make the treasury of his collected essays. It must be remembered that Emerson was in one sense never a student. Books were to him but starting places or stimuli for his thought; his essays and lectures were slow accretions around an original idea; and the men and women about him, life and nature as he read them, were more to him than printed pages. So he had no need of the paraphernalia of the student. He seldom quoted. His books are full of native and homely illustrations that serve to mark one difference between him, our great thinker, and all the philosophers whom Europe and Asia had produced.

The study is very simply decorated. In one corner stands the bust of a dear friend. On the walls are photographs and engravings, some of them mementoes of European acquaintances. Over the black marble fireplace hangs an oil copy of Michelangelo's "Fates", a symbolic picture which could not be more appropriately hung. The furniture is of a good New England period. The room is bright; it expresses, as does the house, the large simplicity and unvarying cheerfulness of the man who for so many years inhabited it.

In one other Concord house did Emerson do his writing, the Antiquarian house, then a boarding-

In Emerson's Study

house to which he escaped when the press of worshipping Transcendentalists broke in too much upon his time.

Behind the Emerson house spread its gardens, where in his earlier period Emerson used to work. Then occurred that friendly rivalry between himself and his wife of which he so quaintly tells: did he plant vegetables, flowers came up in their places. Mrs. Emerson was a lover of gardens; she brought with her from Plymouth many of her favorite plants, and year by year gave their descendants about in the village,—a neighborly habit followed by her admirable daughter, so that many Concord gardens have come, in part, from this Emersonian enclosure. But it was not Mrs. Emerson who drove her husband from the work of gardening. He did not love it. His little Waldo, anxiously watching his father at work, cried, "Papa, I am afraid you'll dig your leg!" The philosopher has given us his own account of the interminableness of the pursuit of weeds. The labor fatigued him. And his conclusion is summed up in the pithy sentence: "The writer shall not dig."

But if we cannot associate Emerson with his garden, except in this negative fashion, we may remember that Thoreau has been busy all about the place. He lived at different periods in the Emerson family, where his aptness at work of all kinds was constantly apparent, and where his host felt great relief at this saving of his labor. Alcott came with assistance of a thoroughly characteristic and less practical kind. At the left of the barn, within a circle of pines which still stands there, the conversationalist built what was intended for a rural study for Emerson, constructed, as was Alcott's way, out of crooked roots and boughs which it was his delight to find in the woods. This material so dominated the architecture that Thoreau, who assisted as capable of driving nails to stay, complained that he felt as if he were nowhere doing nothing. As a study the draughty and mosquito-haunted building was a failure; even its undeniable beauty did not last long, for in order to be picturesque, its thatch curved upward at the eaves, and the whole soon rotted away.

In contrast we may think of the simple gift of Thoreau's elder brother. "John Thoreau, Jr., one day put a blue-bird's box on my barn, — fifteen years ago, it must be, — and there it still is, with every summer a melodious family in it, adorning the place and singing his praises. There's a gift for you which cost the giver no money, but nothing which he bought could have been so good." The blue-bird box has lasted until destroyed by a spring gale of the present year.

Emerson's townsmen appreciated him. "Sam" Staples called him a "first rate neighbor and one who always kept his fences up." The attempt to blackmail him by moving an unsightly building on to the lot before his house met with a prompt response when the young men of the town came in the night and pulled it down. One Concord woman, when asked, "Do you understand Mr. Emerson?" to one of whose lectures she was going, replied: "Not a word, but I like to go and see him stand up there and look as if he thought every one was as good as he was." But a neighboring farmer, who said that he had heard all of Mr. Emerson's Lyceum lectures, added: "and understood 'em, too." And unforgettable is the picture of Concord welcoming Emerson returning from Europe to the house which his neighbors, after its fire, had helped more distant friends to rebuild. They erected for him a triumphal arch, cheered as he passed under it, and accompanied him to his gate. No wonder that his emotion choked him, nor that when he could control his voice he spoke of their common blood — "one family — in Concord."

Old Concord

When it came time for Emerson to die, his work had been done, and well done. Over the whole of the land his uplifting message had taken its full effect. He was a great force during the Civil War. He guided millions of young men and women on their way. Those who had never heard his name knew his message; and the present generation is the wiser and happier for the spread of his spoken and written word. In America, but not in America alone, he stands unique in his influence. When in the spring of 1882 he died, not his town only, but the whole world, mourned.

The constancy of Emerson to his ancestral town is in contrast to the goings and comings of Alcott, at least for a number of years after he first frequented Concord. The prospect of Emerson's neighborhood brought him to the town, where first, before his unfortunate "Fruitlands" venture, he lived in the "Cottage", sometimes called the Hosmer Cottage, on Main Street beyond the railroad bridge. The place, though small, was complete with its numerous little rooms, its barn and sheds. Except for the disappearance of the barn, and the addition of a mansard roof, it looks the same to-day, modestly brown, unobtrusive, and comfortable. In this house were written many of

The Alcott " Cottage " (1840–1842) on Main Street

the charming early letters of Alcott to his children, which, some of them in facsimile to show his drawings or his lettering, have lately been published in such attractive form. And from this house Alcott started on his journey to England, turning at the door to say to his wife that he might have forgotten to pay for his new suit of clothes, which, however, she would attend to, of course.

And the patient woman was wondering how she could feed her family until his return!

The result of his journey was the unlucky "Fruitlands" experiment, which sent the Alcotts back to Concord at the very lowest point of their fortune. The coming of a legacy, however, with some help from Emerson, enabled them to buy the house which Alcott named "Hillside", now known as Hawthorne's "Wayside." A "mean-looking affair" the house was when bought, but Alcott immediately enlarged and improved it. He made terraces on the slope behind the house, planting with grapes and beautifying with summer-houses built in his favorite style of rustic architecture. And for three years this was the home of the happiest part of Louisa Alcott's childhood.

She herself has given some pictures of its fun. One day Emerson and Margaret Fuller came to call. They discussed Alcott's advanced theories of education, and Miss Fuller said:

"'Well, Mr. Alcott, you have been able to carry out your methods in your own family, and I should like to see your model children.'

"She did in a few moments, for as the guests stood on the door steps a wild uproar approached, and round the corner of the house came a wheel-barrow holding baby May arrayed as a queen; I was the horse, bitted and bridled and driven by my elder sister Anna, while Lizzie played dog and barked as loud as her gentle voice permitted.

"All were shouting and wild with fun which, however, came to a sudden end as we espied the stately group before us, for my foot tripped, and down we all went in a laughing heap, while my mother put a climax to the joke by saying with a dramatic wave of the hand:

"'Here are the model children, Miss Fuller.'"

These were the famous days of the Alcott dramatics. Their means were of the simplest; costumes and stage fittings were home-made; even the dramas themselves were often written by the girls. Mrs. Alcott actively assisted, the philosopher placidly approved, and the wholesome circle of girls and boys which the four Alcott children speedily drew round themselves eagerly helped in anything that was undertaken. No reader of *Little Women* needs any further description of this feature of life at Hillside.

Chiefly Literary

No one ever left in Concord pleasanter memories than the four Alcott sisters. In character they varied widely. Anna, the oldest, was domestic and thoughtful, a good home-maker; yet she had a share of Louisa's ability with her pen, wrote quite as many of the home-made dramas, has left fine letters, and it was she (not Louisa) who pinned inside a journal the manuscript of a story of her own, which she read aloud to the family, receiving their hearty approval. Louisa was the tomboy, ready for any prank; she was also ambitious and a hard worker, with a special bent for writing which for many years went unrewarded. Elizabeth was gentle and sweet, of a constitution not weak, but later broken by a severe attack of scarlet fever brought by the mother's devotion to her work among the poor. May, the youngest daughter, had some of Louisa's adventurousness; she rode recklessly when at rare intervals she could secure a mount. Her talent was artistic, and was devotedly improved; she is famous for her copies of Turner. She possessed a large share of the Alcott quality of generosity, and gave practical help to struggling beginners. Together, these four made a household that naturally attracted the young folk of their town.

Old Concord

But no one in the Alcott household could fail of acquaintance with the serious side of life. It may have seemed romantic to shelter fugitive slaves. "My first pupil," wrote Miss Alcott, "was a very black George Washington whom I taught to write on the hearth with charcoal, his big fingers finding pen and pencil unmanageable." Yet the same qualities which led Alcott to take this noble risk, brought him also, and frequently, to the edge of pennilessness. The family shared its dinner with all who came to ask. They took in some sickly wayfarers with the result that the whole family caught small-pox. True, once at least the family generosity was almost immediately justified.

"One snowy Saturday night," writes Miss Alcott, "when our wood was very low, a poor child came to beg a little, as the baby was sick and the father on a spree with all his wages. My mother hesitated at first, as we had also a baby. Very cold weather was upon us, and a Sunday to be got through before more wood could be had. My father said, 'Give half our stock, and trust in Providence; the weather will moderate, or wood will come.' Mother laughed, and answered in her cheery way, 'Well, their need is greater than ours, and if our half gives out, we can go to bed and tell stories.' So a generous half went to the poor neighbor, and a little later in the eve, when the storm still raged and we were about to cover our fire to keep it, a knock came, and a farmer who usually supplied us appeared, saying anxiously,

'I started for Boston with a load of wood, but it drifts so I want to go home. Wouldn't you like to have me drop the wood here; it would accommodate me, and you needn't hurry about paying for it.' 'Yes,' said father; and as the man went off he turned to mother with a look that much impressed us children with his gifts as a seer, 'Didn't I tell you wood would come if the weather did not moderate?' Mother's motto was, 'Hope, and keep busy,' and one of her sayings, 'Cast your bread upon the waters, and after many days it will come back buttered.'"

With such a husband, lovable but unworldly, Mrs. Alcott needed these mottoes. Though Emerson often acted as a Providence, the family was frequently on short commons. But nothing could shake their belief in its head, nor, for that matter, did Emerson waver in his admiration of his friend. He wrote, "Once more for Alcott it may be said that he is sincerely and necessarily engaged to his task, and not wilfully or ostentatiously or pecuniarily."

And Staples, the jailer, gave a similar tribute when he said after he had arrested Alcott for refusal to pay his poll-tax as a protest against the laws: "I vum, I believe it was nothin' but principle, for I never heard a man talk honester."

It was inevitable, however, that the family should get deeper and deeper into difficulties. "The trials of life began about this time," wrote Miss Alcott;

"and my happy childhood ended." The house which saw so much merriment saw also the two older sisters learning to appreciate the burden which lay upon their mother, the duties which they themselves could not escape. Mrs. Alcott's anxieties so preyed upon her that a Boston friend, coming to call, found her unable to conceal the traces of recent tears. "Abby Alcott," demanded the visitor, "what does this mean?" The story being told, she offered Mrs. Alcott employment in Boston.

As was usual, the proposal was taken to the family council. In Boston the father could find more chance to make money; the two older girls were able to teach. "It was an anxious council," wrote Miss Alcott many years after, "and always preferring action to discussion, I took a brisk run over the hill and then settled down for 'a good think' in my favorite retreat. It was an old cart-wheel, half hidden in grass under the locusts where I used to sit to wrestle with my sums. . . . I think I began to shoulder my burden then and there."

That burden she took to Boston, and nine years later she brought it back again. Let any one who supposes Miss Alcott's life was happy, read carefully her letters and journals of those years. There was drudgery at the housekeeping, uncongenial teaching, humiliation from unkind employers, and always the disappointment of continual failure in the work for which she felt herself best fitted. Gradually she came to know that if prosperity was to be won for the family, it must be by her alone. By his famous, but not profitable, "conversations" her father could never hope to keep the family even in bread and butter. With this knowledge, then, in 1857 she came back to Concord, weighed down also by anxiety for the life of her sister.

In Concord, Elizabeth Alcott died, and in Sleepy Hollow cemetery she lies buried. Louisa, who had interrupted her work to nurse her dying sister, now took it up again. Her sister Anna's engagement seemed at first only another bereavement: "I moaned in private," says her journal, "over my great loss." But fifteen years afterward she wrote, "Now that John is dead, I can truly say we all had cause to bless the day he came into the family; for we gained a son and brother, and Anna the best husband ever known." Her writing of imaginative and even lurid tales prospered somewhat; but she was writing for a market that seldom pays well. She wrote a short play, which was produced without either success or failure; she taught again; she tried again the pleasures of dramatics in Concord. The approach of the country toward its years of trial found her intensely interested; and when at last the war broke out, she was anxious to serve as a nurse.

The family was now living in the "Orchard House." "Hillside" had been sold to Mr. Hawthorne. The old house on the new land had been considered useless; but Mr. Alcott proved its timbers to be still sound, and repaired it according to his fancy. The few odd external ornaments and the many individual conveniences inside are of his invention. His daughters did the painting and papering, and May devised and executed the charming decorations which still are there. As to the furnishings, it is pleasant to know that their simplicity, so little in agreement with the fussy taste of the day, but quite in accord with modern ideas, arose as much from Alcott good sense as from Alcott poverty. The great elms in front were the chief beauty of the place; the orchard, in which the whole family took great pleasure, has since disappeared. It is natural that, with the wide changes in their older home, all the early Alcott traditions should cluster around this place. Its simple aspect and comfortable proportions speak of home and hospitality.

Orchard House, Home of the Alcotts

Chiefly Literary

From this house Miss Alcott departed when she received her call to go to the front. "We had all," she says, "been full of courage till the last moment came; then we all broke down. I realized that I had taken my life in my hand, and might never see them all again. I said, 'Shall I stay, Mother?' as I hugged her close. 'No, go! and the Lord be with you!' answered the Spartan woman; and till I turned the corner she bravely smiled and waved her wet handkerchief on the doorstep." It proved that Miss Alcott had indeed taken her life in her hand. A period of arduous nursing resulted in an attack of typhoid pneumonia, which forever took away her elasticity. From that period the physical joy of life departed.

And yet the Alcott success, so long worked for, was now at hand. Her father had already received the approval of his town, by being appointed superintendent of the public schools. His daughter now wrote her *Hospital Sketches*, which were well received by the public. She felt that at last she had found her vein and could be sure of herself. Her powers and her reputation slowly grew, until at last she wrote in her diary:

"September, 1867. — Niles, partner of Roberts, asked me to write a girls' book. Said I'd try."

She tried. The result was *Little Women*.

What would appear to be the first half of the book was written at the Orchard House in the spring and early summer of 1868. "I plod away," she wrote, "though I don't like this sort of thing. Never liked girls or knew many, except my sisters; but our queer plays and experiences may prove interesting, though I doubt it."

No wonder that, years afterward, she wrote against this entry in her journal, "Good joke." The publisher's test of the book was made by giving the manuscript into the hands of a girl whose absorbed interest, whose laughter and tears, were sufficient proof of its quality. The second part of the book was begun in November. "Girls write to ask who the little women marry, as if that was the only end and aim of a woman's life. I *won't* marry Jo to Laurie to please any one."

And so at last the "pathetic family," as she called it, came into its own. She might, in a letter home, crow about "the Alcotts, who can't make money." Her "rumpled soul" was soothed by the thought (and in it we can see the extent of her absorption in her family) that "we made our own money ourselves."

But the cost was very great. The drain of overwork and the habit of industry often made mere existence a burden. Though from this time her books for young people were the delight of the nation, she wrote with continual weariness. Yet no hint of this feeling crept into her pages, or dulled the vivacity of her tales. The habit of daily heroism prevented.

Through childhood, Miss Alcott had longed for a room of her own. She had received it at "Hillside." Her father, all through his life till now, had wished to found a School of Philosophy, and now at last it was made possible. At one side of the Alcott place, well to the left of Orchard House as one views it from the road, was built the simple but not unpicturesque building which in the summer of 1880 delighted Alcott's heart with its school of thirty pupils and its many more visitors. There was much lecturing; the town and the country were amused; and Miss Alcott, not for the first time, in the midst of the extra work which he threw upon her, derived innocent entertainment from her guileless father. The school existed for only a few years. The building has been removed, and its influence has departed; but it was for more than twenty years one of the Concord sights.

Louisa Alcott's burdens began to grow too great

for her. Her mother had died; her sister May, after the short term of her European marriage, died also, and sent to Concord the baby daughter to be her aunt's solace and care. The little family moved to the Thoreau house on Main Street, where they lived with the widowed sister. Here, or in Boston where she also used to stay, with difficulty Miss Alcott finished her remaining stories. Many claims on her sympathy and purse came to her, often from perfect strangers, and in her nervous state these kept her at work. But her father was placid to the end. The big study which was built for him still contains his books and his many journals; the pictures and furnishings of the house still speak the Alcott taste; and the simplicity of the building reminds of the plain virtues of a family at which we can only wonder. They passed away. Alcott died in Boston on March 4, 1888. On the morning of his funeral his famous daughter, then living at her physician's in Roxbury, followed him to rest.

Of the Alcott family, the world remembers two for their achievements. Their town remembers more. For patience and hard work in difficulties, for unwavering purpose in developing their talents, for strong family feeling, a brave front to the world, neighborliness, and ungrudging generosity, in Concord the Alcotts will never be forgotten.

We have seen that Alcott's "Hillside" became the property of Hawthorne, who changed its name to "Wayside." After seven years spent away from Concord, chiefly in Salem, Lenox, and West Newton, Hawthorne returned, in 1852, and occupied the house, unchanged in form from Alcott's day. A letter of his wife describes her arrival in advance of his, the drying of mattresses wet while moving, the nailing down of the carpet lining, and the "admirable effect" of the woodwork, "painted in oak." He enjoyed the place, cut his beanpoles in the woods, sold his hay, was rather unappreciative of his farming land across the road, and rightly anticipated that his waste land on the hilltop behind would yield him the true interest on his investment. Alcott's terraces he let grow up with trees. And perhaps remembering his own vision, as expressed in one of his prefaces, expecting here to see it fulfilled, he named the place "Wayside." He had written: "I sat down by the wayside of life, like a man under enchantment, and a shrubbery sprang up around me, and the bushes grew to be saplings, and the saplings became trees, until no exit appeared possible, through the entangling depths of my obscurity." And truly the vision pictures his mental life at this place.

Hawthorne's great books were not written in Concord. All he accomplished in his first tenancy of the new house was *Tanglewood Tales,* and a campaign biography of his friend Pierce. We know that at this time his health was good, that he picnicked in the woods with his family, and saw his neighbors as little as he could. He had no plans for going away; but Pierce's election to the Presidency led to the offer of the consulate at Liverpool, and Hawthorne accepted it. He left in 1853, not to return until the summer of 1860. He brought for his final sojourn a wide acquaintance with people, which at last made him accustomed to meet strangers. His new book, the *Marble Faun,* had placed him at the summit of his fame. But his physical health had broken.

Coming with many literary plans, he wished to secure himself a quiet study. So besides other alterations he built the "tower" which is the striking feature of "Wayside." Different as the house is from the Manse in its lack of seclusion, the tower nevertheless gives a certain suggestion of inaccessibility. Besides, the mysterious woods creep close. Even here there is that romantic aloofness which Hawthorne's nature always created.

Hawthorne's "Wayside"

Chiefly Literary

In the house, the tower-study is the strongest reminder of him. "A staircase, narrow and steep," wrote his son, "ascends through the floor, the opening being covered by a sort of gabled structure, to one end of which a standing desk was affixed; a desk table was placed against the side. The room was about twenty feet square, with four gables, and the ceiling, instead of being flat, was a four-sided vault, following the conformation of the roof. There were five windows, the southern and eastern ones opening upon a flat tin roof, upon which one might walk or sit in suitable weather. The walls were papered with paper of a light golden hue, without figures. There was a closet for books on each side of the northern window, which looked out upon the hill. A small fireplace, to which a stove was attached, was placed between the two southern windows. The room was pleasant in autumn and spring; but in winter the stove rendered the air stifling, and in summer the heat of the sun was scarcely endurable. Hawthorne, however, spent several hours a day in his study, and it was there that the *Old Home* was written, and *Septimius Felton*, and *Dr. Grimshawe*, and the Dolliver fragment."

Howells, coming on the same visit on which he

saw Emerson, called also upon Hawthorne at "Wayside," and has given a pleasant picture of the great romancer. But Alcott, living next door, has his own word to say of his neighbor's shyness and desire to avoid notice. The truth was that though his consular experiences had fitted Hawthorne to meet people when necessary, the natural gloom of his nature was pressing on him now, accentuated by both his own declining health and the great crisis through which the nation was passing. Pierce, to whose administration was laid the blame of the coming of the Civil War, was very unpopular; and as Pierce's friend, Hawthorne felt the situation keenly. Brooding, he found himself unfit for work. He retired often to his hilltop toward the close of the day; and pacing up and down along the crest, he wore the path of which the traces still exist. His daughter wrote: "We could catch sight of him going back and forth up there, with now and then a pale blue gleam of sky among the trees, against which his figure passed clear. . . . Along this path in spring huddled pale blue violets, of a blue that held sunlight, pure as his own eyes. . . . My father's violets were the wonder of the year for us."

His literary motives in these last years were in part connected with his house. Thoreau had told him that it had once been inhabited by a man who believed he should never die. The idea took hold of Hawthorne, and he seemed unable to escape from it. From England he had brought the motive of a bloody footstep. Both of these he wrought into *Septimius Felton*, the scene of which was laid in the house and (as we have seen) on the hilltop behind. Earthly immortality was to have taken a large part in the *Dolliver Romance*, which he began, and the first part of which he published, but which was never finished. For Hawthorne's own death was drawing near.

His decline came visibly. His once black hair began to turn white. He was thinner, paler, stooped a little, and his vigorous step became slow. A trip toward the south bringing him only the shock of the sudden death of his companion, he started with Pierce to the White Mountains. And it is appropriate that of him, who dwelt so persistently upon the idea of death, we should have two clear pictures of his children's farewells.

"A few days before he and Pierce set forth," wrote his son, "I came up to Concord from Cambridge to make some requests of him. I remained only an hour, having to take the afternoon train back to college. He was sitting in the bedroom upstairs; my mother and my two sisters were there also. It was a pleasant morning in early May. I made my request (whatever it was) and, after listening to the ins and outs of the whole matter, he acceded to it. I had half anticipated refusal, and was the more gratified. I said good-by, and went to the door, where I stood a moment looking back into the room. He was standing at the foot of the bed, leaning against it, and looking at me with a smile. He had on his old dark coat; his hair was almost wholly white, and he was very pale. But the expression of his face was one of beautiful kindness, — the gladness of having done me a pleasure, and perhaps something more, that I did not then know of."

His daughter described him as he left for his journey. "Like a snow image of an unbending but an old, old man, he stood for a moment gazing at me. My mother sobbed, as she walked beside him to the carriage. We have missed him in the sunlight, in the storm, in the twilight, ever since."

Hawthorne never returned from his journey. He died at Plymouth, New Hampshire, in the night of May 18–19, 1864, peacefully in his sleep. His body lies buried in Sleepy Hollow cemetery. Among his trees near "Wayside" a simple memorial was erected to him on the centenary of his birth.

Beyond "Wayside", and close at hand, stands the little cottage of Ephraim Wales Bull, the originator of the Concord grape. He came to Concord to carry on his trade of a gold-beater; he had a little workshop and kept several workmen. But as time went on, his taste for horticulture caused him to interrupt the more lucrative business for the pursuit of a favorite desire, the breeding of a grape which should be earlier and hardier than any then in cultivation, since the grapes of his day, chief among them the Catawba and Isabella, gave very poor results in New England. He had the patience and skill of the true originator. Finding in his grounds a wild grape of somewhat superior flavor, he crossed it with the Isabella, and saved the fruit. "I put these grapes," he said, "whole, into the ground, skin and all, at a depth of two inches, about the first of October, after they had thoroughly ripened, and covered the row with boards. I nursed these seedlings for six years, and of the large number only one proved worth the saving. On the 10th of September, 1849, I was enabled to pick a bunch of grapes, and when I showed them to a neighbor, who tasted them, he at once exclaimed, 'Why, this is better than the Isabella!'"

From this grape, which he named the Concord, Bull gained fame, and but very little money. He had not the business knowledge of the nurserymen, into whose pockets passed most of the profits from this and other grapes which the horticulturist bred. The result was that he died in poverty, though never neglected. He held as a result of his reputation several elective or appointive offices, and was always much respected. Personally he was a man of oddities. He had a formidable temper; occasionally at the Hawthornes' could be heard the distant sound of his tremendous wrath. When in public life, he wore a silk hat, shaved carefully, and wore a wig of glossy yellow-brown hair. But when he retired, "a transformation occurred almost as startling as those in a theatre, and he appeared as an aged man with snow white beard, nearly bald, oftenest seen in a dressing gown and little black silk cap, tending his plants lovingly." He died in 1895 and is buried near his famous neighbor. The best memorial of him is the ancient original grapevine, still to be seen by its trellis, near the little Grapevine Cottage.

Lexington Road leads on to Meriam's Corner, where the tablet in the wall marks the beginning of the running fight with the British. From this place one can almost see, up the old road to Bedford and beyond the Meriam homestead, the site

Academy Lane

of Thoreau's birthplace. But the house has been moved away, and indeed it would be difficult to limit one's memories of Thoreau's early years to the confines of a house. His strong taste for an outdoor life possessed him through his youth, and steadily growing stronger after his college days, at last made it impossible for him to live the conventional life. He did indeed make the first venture common to the young college graduate — school-teaching. In the old schoolhouse on the Square he tried this profession, though on the new principle of avoiding corporal punishment. But for those days this was too ideal. The school committee complained. Thoreau tried their method by whipping a half dozen scholars on the same day, and that night sent in his resignation because his arrangements had been interfered with. He then taught with his brother John in the new Concord Academy, the site of which is recalled by the name of the street on which it stood, Academy Lane. Here, though he was happier, he was not free, and so turned away from the work.

His life at the Emerson house allowed him the desultory employment which he preferred, giving him time to himself. But as more and more he desired complete independence, so he experimented toward the means for it. He found that by a few weeks' labor in the year (oftenest at surveying) he could satisfy his simple needs : plain food, serviceable clothes, a book or two, and nothing more. It must not be supposed that he ever desired to emancipate himself from human society; he enjoyed it too much, and never made a move toward avoiding his friends. Indeed, in spite of his strong taste for solitude, he had an equally strong affection for his family and his town. Concord was enough for him to judge the world by. When once, while he was still a boy, his mother suggested that some day he would buckle on his knapsack and roam abroad, his eyes filled with tears, and he was comforted only by his sister's saying : "No, Henry, you shall not go; you shall stay at home and live with us." Stay at home in one sense he did not, yet in another sense he did. He was never long happy away from Concord.

So when in 1845 he made his famous experiment at Walden, he did not mean entirely to escape from society. He knew very well the shortest route home, and often took it. "I went to the woods," he wrote, "because I wished to live deliberately, to front only the essential facts of life, and see if I could learn what it had to teach, and not, when I came to die, discover that I had not lived."

Chiefly Literary

Walden, which lies by road less than two miles from Concord village, is an irregular pond of some sixty-four acres, now, as then, completely surrounded by woods. Campers and the railroad have brought fires to the woodland, and the gipsy moth has necessitated much cutting; therefore the pond is not so beautiful as in Thoreau's day. But the dominating bluffs are the same, and the place seems still remote. Here on Emerson's land, above a placid cove, Thoreau built the hut whose site is marked by the cairn of stones; the boards he bought from an Irishman's shanty; Alcott, Hawthorne, Curtis, and others helped him to erect the frame; the furnishings he largely made himself, and he settled there before summer. His steadiest employment was on the beanfield which he planted near the road; his real pursuit was in observing the life of the fields and woods.

"Snakes," said Emerson, "coiled round his leg, the fishes swam into his hand, and he took them out of the water; he pulled the woodchuck out of his hole by the tail, and took the foxes under his protection from the hunters." Once, when a sparrow alighted on his shoulder, he felt it "a greater honor than any epaulet he could have worn." He studied the fish, the loons on the lake, the ants in his woodpile. In the pages of his *Walden*, and in his later essays, these things are charmingly reflected.

Friends came to see him at his hut. He speaks oftenest of Channing and Alcott, but others came as well, not always to his satisfaction. To such as did not know when their visit had ended, he gave a broad hint by leaving them, answering them "from greater and greater remoteness."

It is fairly certain that the hut at Walden was a station for the underground railway. "It offers advantages," he wrote, "which it may not be good policy to divulge." But whether or not Thoreau harbored slaves here, we have a picture of him in this employment at a later period. "I sat and watched the singular and tender devotion of the scholar to the slave. He must be fed, his swollen feet bathed, and he must think of nothing but rest. Again and again this coolest and calmest of men drew near to the trembling negro, and bade him feel at home, and have no fear that any power should again wrong him. He could not walk this day, but must mount guard over the fugitive."

During his Walden period, Thoreau had his brief experience with the law. Like Alcott at an earlier day, he had refused to pay his poll-tax, in protest

Thoreau's Cairn at Walden

against the Mexican War. Going to the village to have a shoe mended, he was arrested and put in jail, where Emerson hastened to him.

"Henry, why are you here?"

"Why are you not here?" was Thoreau's rejoinder. He took his imprisonment calmly, was interested in the new experience, placidly accepted his release on the morrow because some one had paid his fine, and presently was leading a huckleberry party to a hilltop from which "the State was nowhere to be seen."

Thoreau left Walden at the end of two years, and lived at the Emerson house for nearly two years more, during part of which the philosopher was in Europe. Then for the rest of his life, Thoreau lived in the house which his father, with his aid, rebuilt on the main street. Literary success came to him; he was widely known, and had new congenial acquaintances. But he still lived an individual life. He tramped the fields as he had always done, frequented farmhouses in his study of human nature, led the children to the woods, or, in the village street, made them hear the vireo's song which till then they had not noticed. He interested himself, but only spasmodically, in his father's pencil-making, which was done in the ell of the house. Having improved the machine for grinding the lead, and after learning to make a perfect pencil, he gave up the work, — it could teach him nothing more. In the attic of the house he kept his collections of eggs, flowers, and Indian relics, and here he did his writing. The house was smaller then, for Alcott had not added his study; the interior has since been much changed. But in this house Thoreau felt the strong culminating passion of his life.

As the slavery question pressed more and more upon the country, Thoreau felt it as deeply affecting him. John Brown came to Concord, and the naturalist was impassioned for his cause. The two had a long talk together, in the Main Street house. Brown's attempt at Harper's Ferry and his imprisonment drew from Thoreau the strong "Plea for Captain John Brown" which he repeated at many places. Never did Thoreau come more out of himself than at this time. His critics had reproached him with coldness and aloofness, but now he showed himself entirely human.

It was the last great chapter of the experience with life which he had so ardently desired. Exposure in the woods brought on a serious illness, from which even his vigorous frame never recovered. Consumption slowly wasted him away. His dying was

like some of the heroic endurances of his outdoor
life, and he studied it in the same way. He was
cheerful, he bore sleeplessness well, and he vividly
described the dreams that came in his fitful repose.
When he could no longer climb the stairs, he had his
bed brought down to the parlor that looked upon
the street, in order to see the passers-by. His
famous friends came to see him; and when in their
awe of the sick man the children did not come, he
asked for them. "I love them as if they were my
own." So they, as well as his older friends, made
his sick bed pleasant. In his last letter he wrote,
"I am enjoying existence as much as ever, and regret nothing." In May, 1862, very peacefully he
died.

Beyond this Main Street house (where cling those
sadder memories of Thoreau which can be associated
with his indoor life) on Elm Street, and bordering the
river, stands the picturesque residence of Frank
B. Sanborn, a younger contemporary of Concord's
great men. Coming to Concord in 1855, at the request of Emerson and several other citizens who
desired a superior school for their children, he
taught here for eight years, and has resided here for
most of the remaining time. He was a leader in the
joyous dramatics in which the Alcott sisters and his

own scholars took such happy part. He was well acquainted with the notable men, accounts of whom he has passed on to us. In the days when to be an abolitionist had its dangers, Mr. Sanborn became prominent as the friend of John Brown. Brown twice visited him in Concord, once in a house owned by Channing, then standing opposite Thoreau's, and once in the house directly behind the Thoreau house, which during recent years has been occupied as a girls' school. Mr. Sanborn was one of those northern men who were aware that Brown was preparing some movement for the freeing of the slaves, and who were providing him with money.

As a consequence, after the Harper's Ferry raid occurred that incident in Concord of which the newspapers of the day were very full, — Mr. Sanborn's attempted abduction. Officers sent by the Sergeant-at-arms of the United States Senate surprised him in his house at night, showed a warrant, and tried to force him into a carriage. Though handcuffed, he resisted stoutly, and his sister's calls brought help. The neighbors prevented the success of the attempt; and Judge Hoar, hearing the noise and guessing its cause, had already started to fill out a writ of *habeas corpus* before a summons came for him to do so. The sheriff presented the writ to

The Sanborn House from the River

the officers, who, after the rough handling they had had, were glad to give up their prisoner. Legal means prevented the repetition of the event.

Mr. Sanborn was for years in the employ of the State of Massachusetts; he has long been associated with the *Springfield Republican* as editor and correspondent; he has edited the works of others, and has published his own poems and writings. During the life of the School of Philosophy, he was its secretary, and was also a lecturer in it. That shy genius, Ellery Channing, spent the last years of his life in Mr. Sanborn's home. The building Mr. Sanborn erected for himself; with its dark front and tangled shrubbery it seems as withdrawn as Hawthorne's own. From the "three-arched stone bridge" that stands close by, the stepped brick end of the tall house seems to stand somberly above the quiet river. "The last of the Concord School," as Mr. Sanborn is often called, is easily recognized in Concord streets by his tall, stooping figure, his white locks, and his rapid stride.

The limits of this survey of Concord allow no room for other houses, whether of local or more general interest. Neither is it here possible to do much more than to indicate the charm of the old streets. Concord was not planned: it grew, and its roads seldom run straight for more than a little distance. The half-mile of Main Street beginning at the Library gives almost the longest vista uninterrupted by rise or turn; under its arching trees the wide road is, winter or summer, very beautiful. Elsewhere the roads meander gently, following the slight contours of the ground; they are generously broad, comfortably shaded. In spite of the fact that Concord's site was chosen because of its meadows, it is only in the center of the town that there is any uniformity of level. The undulations of the roads, therefore, add another charm. Besides the elms that line them, the streets are edged by the shrubberies and hedges of residences that show the simple variations of colonial architecture. Outside the town the meadows, cultivated fields, and woods, always with glimpses of gently rising hills, give varied views. If in America there is anything that speaks simply and feelingly of the older times, it is a New England town. Concord, — dignified, picturesque, homelike, and still vital, — is notable among its kind.

The Burying Grounds

IV

IN any town as old as Concord, the graves naturally attract attention, from the interest either
in stones recording famous names, or in the memorials of forgotten dead whose epitaphs are odd
or quaint. Concord's two older cemeteries, on
Main Street and on the hill, have abundant interest
of the latter kind.

These two enclosures traditionally contend for
priority; but since the earlier graves for many
years had no stones at all, this matter cannot be
settled except by the conjecture that the earlier
burials took place upon the hill, near the original
church. Both of these cemeteries contain stones
of the seventeenth century, bearing the names of
old Concord families.

In those early days, and for a long time afterward,
people were more given to epitaphs than we are now.

The virtues of the departed were impressed upon the reader, sometimes with an incongruity that provokes a smile. Mr. Job Brooks, who died at ninety-one, was cautiously "considered by survivors as having come to the grave in a full age." His wife "lived with her said husband upward of sixty-five years, and died in the hope of a resurrection to a better life." Tilly Merrick "had an excellent art in family government." The pompous epitaph is excellently displayed on the tombstone of James Minot, "Esq. A. M.," for here it is stated that he was "An excelling grammarian; enriched with the gift of prayer and preaching; a commanding officer; a physician of great value; a great lover of peace as well as of justice; and which was his greatest glory, a gent'n of distinguished virtue and goodness, happy in a virtuous posterity; and, living religiously, died comfortably, September 20, 1735, aged 83."

Yet on the other hand there are here inscriptions which by their simple recital of manly traits bear conviction with them. Such is the case with the epitaph of the son of the foregoing, Timothy Minot, schoolmaster and licensed preacher. "He was a preacher of the gospel whose praise was in all the churches: a school-master in Concord for many years: his actions were governed by the dictates of his conscience; he was a lover of peace; given to hospitality; a lover of good men; sober, just, temperate; a faithful friend, a good neighbour, an excellent husband, a tender, affectionate parent, and a good master."

Besides these claims to virtue, the old stones frequently bear moral sentiments or serious reflections, always best in the form of quotations from the Bible. But our ancestors felt also the attractiveness of poetry, and in Concord cemeteries we have many examples of the species of sacred doggerel which was almost stereotyped for generations, but of which there are amusing variations. Thus little Charlotty Ball says:

> "My dady and my mamy dears, dry up your tears,
> Here I must lie till Christ appears."

and Archibald Smith, a Baptist, takes occasion to suggest his "persuasion" in the verse:

> "The just shall, from their mouldering dust,
> Ascend the mansions of the blest,
> Where Paul and Silas and John the Baptist
> And all the saints forever rest."

In interest the Hill Burying-ground surpasses the cemetery on Main Street. It has first the advantage that here are buried men of more importance in the town. Here lie those early pastors of Concord, Daniel Bliss, William Emerson, and Ezra Ripley; here are the graves of some of the town's benefactors, John Beaton, Doctor Cuming, and Hugh Cargill; and here also are buried those two heroes of the Fight, Barrett who gave the order to attack the British, and Buttrick who executed it. But apart from this, the little cemetery has the advantage of picturesqueness. As one climbs to the summit of the ridge, the stony path, the tall slender trees, the ordered stones, all pointing upward, make a symbolic composition not readily forgotten. Or from the top, looking downward, one sees first the quaint table-tombs of the old worthies, the rows of graves, and then through the trees, — best shown when these are leafless, — reminders of the living world: the Square and Milldam with their groups of people, the First Parish Meeting-house, and St. Bernard's Church. Thus very near to life, yet with the peace of the other world, the old cemetery lures with its contrasts.

But one stone, humbly set apart, brings more visitors to this spot than do its other interests or beauties. It marks the grave of a man insignificant in his life, and remembered only for an epitaph which has been more widely quoted and translated than has any other of Concord's literary works

except the writings of Emerson. It was penned by
Emerson's great-uncle, Daniel Bliss the Tory.

In the days when the struggle of the Revolution
was drawing near, and when Bliss saw his hopes of
his future vanishing away in the new doctrines of
liberty, there died in Concord a negro who had but
recently been a slave. With a cynicism showing no
tenderness for the man, Bliss made him immortal
by an epitaph. It contained a satire on the times,
on freedom, on human nature itself. People study
it to-day for its clear antithesis and cutting phrases;
but we may remember too that it throws a light
upon one feature of our country's history, also that
it reflects the bitter feeling of a disappointed man.

God wills us free, man wills us slaves.
I will as God wills, God's will be done.
Here lies the body of
JOHN JACK
A native of Africa who died
March 1773, aged about sixty years.
Tho' born in a land of slavery
He was born free.
Tho' he lived in a land of liberty
He lived a slave.
Till by his honest, tho' stolen labors,
He acquired the source of slavery,
Which gave him his freedom,
Tho' not long before
Death the grand tyrant,

Old Concord

Gave him his final emancipation,
And set him on a footing with kings.
Tho' a slave to vice
He practised those virtues
Without which kings are but slaves.

The grave of John Jack lies over the top of the lower part of the ridge, and can be found by following the worn track which branches where the main path turns to climb to the summit. It has always been an object of interest; the early weather-worn stone was replaced; and in antislavery days the grave was tended, as if it were a symbol of the fortunes of the down-trodden race, by Miss Mary Rice, whose house stands not far from the rear of the cemetery. It was this spinster who planted the lilies which yearly, by their blossoms, recall not only the slave, but also the devoted lady and the cause for which she worked.

Concord's most famous cemetery is Sleepy Hollow. From the Square it is reached by Bedford Street, going past, or through, an older burying-ground. Beyond this for many years the hollow lay in natural beauty, its amphitheater a farmer's field, its steep surrounding ridges wooded. The name of Sleepy Hollow was early given it; nature-lovers took pleasure in it, and it was a favorite re-

The Burying Grounds

sort of Concord writers. In especial, Hawthorne was fond of it. "I sat down to-day," he wrote during his stay at the Manse, " . . . in Sleepy Hollow. . . . The present season, a thriving field of Indian corn, now in its most perfect growth, and tasseled out, occupies nearly half the hollow; and it is like the lap of bounteous nature, filled with breadstuff." He writes elsewhere of meeting there Margaret Fuller and Emerson. And he and his wife looked forward fondly to a time when they might build themselves a "castle" on the steepest ridge. He lies there buried now, on the very spot.

In 1855 the Hollow and adjoining land were taken for a cemetery. Wisely, the laying out was very simple. At the formal dedication, Emerson made an address, Channing read a dedicatory poem, and an ode by Frank B. Sanborn was sung — truly prophetic in its lines:

"These waving woods, these valleys low,
 Between these tufted knolls,
Year after year shall dearer grow,
 To many loving souls."

Its half century of age and clustering associations have made Sleepy Hollow celebrated throughout America.

Whether one approaches through the older ceme-

tery or direct from Bedford Street, the entrance to
the Hollow is peculiarly pleasing. Two ridges face
each other like a gateway, guarding a little rise of
the road; from a little distance one notices between
them a line of treetops; then almost abruptly the
Hollow opens to the view, — right, left, and beneath.
The steep nearer bank at first conceals the level of
the amphitheater, which lies in a long, irregular oval,
in full sun. Peaceful it is as when, many years ago,
the name was given it; the curving lines of graves
do but mark its quietude as permanent, and em-
phasize the appropriateness of its name. The two
protecting ridges sweep around it from both sides;
their tall trees enhance the seclusion. Their lines
lead the wandering eye finally to a closer attention of
what at first sight the visitor considers merely as the
attractive completion of the enclosing hills, — the opposite ridge, which rises finely from its screen of hemlocks at the bottom to the tops of its crowning pines.

But then one sees that the ridge is thickly marked
with graves. The broken hemlock cover reveals
their stones; they show above it through the boles
of the taller trees. An indented line of stones
stands along the crest of the hill, marking that
Ridge Path to which, after his first long study is
satisfied, the visitor turns his steps.

Hawthorne's Grave in Sleepy Hollow Cemetery

The Burying Grounds

The road to the left is Hawthorne's cart-track. From it one looks along the solemn Hollow, or back at the dark tomb in the entrance ridge. It was by this road that Hawthorne sat, to listen to the birds in the trees above, or in imagination to build his castle on the hill that steeply rose in front.

As one climbs the path from the Hollow, Hawthorne's grave is the first to be seen at the crest. It lies in a retirement like his own through life, within a cedar hedge. Below, through the trees, the Hollow shows distant and withdrawn : it was thus in life that he viewed the world, and thus his spirit could view it still. Across the path are to be seen, on the very edge of the descent, the several graves of the Thoreau family, their names and dates of birth and death upon one common stone, with small headstones to mark the resting-places of Henry and his less famous relatives. Near by are the stones of the Alcotts, those of the parents and three younger daughters side by side, and of the elder sister and her husband, John Pratt, in an adjoining lot. Here, then, in a space of but a few square rods, lie at rest these three families of friends and neighbors, associated in death as in life.

Further along Ridge Path is the grave of Emerson. Under tall pines it is marked by a great fragment of

rose quartz, on whose face is a modest bronze tablet
with his own couplet,

> "The passive master lent his hand
>   To the vast Soul which o'er him planned."

Within the plot where the body of the master lies
are grouped the gravestones of his family: his
mother and his famous aunt, his "hyacinthine boy"
who died in childhood, and the daughter who tended
his old age. And studying these, one sees here re-
vived the ancient custom of inscribing epitaphs.
Their stately phrases establish the worth of lives of
simple dignity and usefulness; one cannot but pon-
der on them.

Read some of these striking words. Of Emerson's
mother: "Her grand-children who learned their
letters at her knee remember her as a serene and
serious presence, her sons regarded her with entire
love and reverence, and in the generation to which
she belonged it was said of her that she resembled
a vessel laid up unto the Lord, of polished gold
without and full of heavenly manna within." Of
his aunt: "She gave high counsels — it was the
privilege of certain boys to have this immeasurably
high standard indicated to their childhood, a bless-
ing which nothing else in education could supply."

The Burying Grounds

Of his wife: "The love and care for her husband and children was her first earthly interest, but with overflowing compassion her heart went out to the slave, the sick, and the dumb creation. She remembered them that were in bonds as bound with them." And of the daughter still so affectionately remembered in Concord: "She loved her Town. She lived the simple and hardy life of old New England, but exercised a wide and joyful hospitality, and she eagerly helped others. Of a fine mind, she cared more for persons than books, and her faith drew out the best in those around her."

This striking group of memorial stones, of him who needs no epitaph and of those whose lives were worthy of such praise, is scarcely to be equaled anywhere in America. It makes evident what is often forgotten, — the human relationships of the great philosopher. And this noble family becomes a lofty type of what is best in our American homes of simple tastes, quiet lives, and high ideals.

Another Concord family, the Hoars, buried close by at the foot of the ridge, is remarkable for its record of public service. Their graves lie clustered about the massive monument of Samuel Hoar, who during his early life was the acknowledged leader of the Middlesex Bar. In his later years, after serving a term in Congress, he gave himself up to political and philanthropic services. His best remembered act was his journey to Charleston, South Carolina, in 1844, to protest in the name of Massachusetts against regulations affecting free colored seamen. In the public excitement thus occasioned, his life was in danger, but he bore himself with calm courage and wise judgment. Around him lie buried his daughter Elizabeth, the friend of Emerson and many notable people, a woman whose intellect and character were perhaps as fine as any that Concord has produced; his son George Frisbie, for many years United States Senator from Massachusetts; and also his son Ebenezer Rockwood, best known as Judge Hoar, a member of Grant's cabinet, and famous for his public spirit, legal wisdom, and flashing wit. And here once more are modern epitaphs worth study. Other members of this family, who continued its record of ability and public service, lie buried elsewhere in the cemetery. Concord remembers that these men, besides being of national importance, were devoted to its local needs. It is families such as these that have made our American institutions what they are, and have maintained the highest ideals of public service.

The gravestone of Ephraim Wales Bull, the orig-

The Ridge in Sleepy Hollow Cemetery

inator of the Concord grape, is not far from this enclosure of the Hoars.

Apart from the interest in Sleepy Hollow which arises from its famous graves, there is another, its beauty. Its natural advantages have been made the most of in its roads and paths; they have even been gradually improved. There are handsome monuments in the cemetery. Unquestionably the finest is the Melvin memorial, sculptured by Daniel C. French, erected to commemorate four Concord brothers, all soldiers in the Civil War.

To see Sleepy Hollow most intimately one should go when it is undisturbed by human voice. When the early sun casts long shadows, when the dusk is stealing on, when the unbroken expanse of snow lies level above the graves — these are the times when the silence of the place is vocal to the thoughtful ear.

Yet if one would see the cemetery at its most impressive, let him go on Decoration Day, when the place is thronged, when the cannon boom their minute guns, and when the veterans of two wars, with flags and melancholy bugles, come with wreaths of flowers to pay tribute to the comrades that have gone before.

Envoi

ENVOI

IT may sometimes seem, to those inclined to criticize, that Concord has been unduly favored, or that being so, it has plumed itself too greatly on advantages that now are past. It is of course unique to have so many memorials in one small area. The battle-field, the houses of literary interest, Walden with its unusual story, and the famous graves, — it would be indeed remarkable if any town should not boast itself of these. But Concord is not living on its past; it has its present interests, and is attending to them. The tide of tourists little disturbs the business of its streets. And Concord feels as others do who look back to achievements separated from the present by such wide intervals. They are no longer local. Time has made them common property.

One studying the earlier generations finds good

material in Concord, that is all. The hardships and the courage of the founders have left here pathetic and inspiring reminders. The deeds of our ancestors who freed us have their memorial here. Here too those great in thought and literary art have carved their message deep. And there is more. The voiceless generations have left their footprints in this place, so that from the earliest times till now the student can trace their progress in all ways that affect human comfort and happiness. Here we have, then, compressed, condensed, those typical events which make the life of that essential factor in the progress of the New World, an American town.

The present is (and speaking generally the present always will be) crowded with critical problems pressing to be solved. We never shall find safer guidance for their solution than in a study of the past. In Concord, among so many noble memories, earnest lovers of America will find inspiration for the duties and decisions of to-day.

Index

INDEX

Index

Index

Index

Town Hall, 4, 9, 16, 25, 37, 51, 52, 80.
Town Pump, 16.
Two Brothers' Rock, 32.

UNDERGROUND RAILWAY IN CONCORD, 12, 13, 146.
Unitarian Church, 4, 7, 9, 16, 19, 25, 39, 42, 80, 162.

WALDEN POND, 10, 12, 144, 145–149, 175.

"Walden Pond Association", 85.
Walden Street, 38, 84.
Warming pan, 21.
Warren, Joseph, 44.
"Wayside", 84, 117, 124, 131, 132, 133, 135, 138.
Willard, Simon, 27, 33, 40.
White, Deacon, 21, 22, 23.
Wood, Ephraim, 41, 72.
Wright, Amos, 52, 53.
Wright Tavern, 4, 5–6, 16, 37, 38, 46, 47, 80.

www.ingramcontent.com/pod-product-compliance
Lightning Source LLC
Chambersburg PA
CBHW031256090426
42742CB00007B/473

9780809531479